WESLEY AND THE WESLEYANS

Wesley and the Wesleyans challenges the cherished myth that at the moment when the Enlightenment and the Industrial Revolution were threatening the soul of eighteenth-century England, an evangelical revival – led by the Wesleys – saved it. It will interest anyone concerned with the history of Methodism and the Church of England, the evangelical tradition, and eighteenth-century religious thought and experience.

The book starts from the assumption that there was no large-scale religious revival during the eighteenth century. Instead, the role of what is called 'primary religion' – the normal human search for ways of drawing supernatural power into the private life of the individual – is analysed in terms of the emergence of the Wesleyan societies from the Church of England. The Wesleys' achievements are reassessed; there is a fresh, unsentimental description of the role of women in the movement; and an unexpectedly sympathetic picture emerges of Hanoverian Anglicanism.

JOHN KENT is Emeritus Professor of Theology, University of Bristol. His many publications include *Holding the Fort: Studies in Victorian Revivalism* (1978), *The End of the Line?: The Development of Theology since 1700* (1982), *The Unacceptable Face: The Modern Historian and the Church* (1987) and *William Temple: Church, State and Society in Britain, 1880–1950* (1993).

WESLEY
AND THE WESLEYANS

JOHN KENT

CAMBRIDGE
UNIVERSITY PRESS

PUBLISHED BY THE PRESS SYNDICATE OF THE UNIVERSITY OF CAMBRIDGE
The Pitt Building, Trumpington Street, Cambridge, United Kingdom

CAMBRIDGE UNIVERSITY PRESS
The Edinburgh Building, Cambridge CB2 2RU, UK
40 West 20th Street, New York, NY 10011-4211, USA
477 Williamstown Road, Port Melbourne, VIC 3207, Australia
Ruiz de Alarcón 13, 28014 Madrid, Spain
Dock House, The Waterfront, Cape Town 8001, South Africa

http://www.cambridge.org

First published 2002

Printed in the United Kingdom at the University Press, Cambridge

Typeface Fournier 12.5/14 pt   *System* LaTeX 2$_\varepsilon$ [TB]

A catalogue record for this book is available from the British Library

ISBN 0 521 45532 4 hardback
ISBN 0 521 45555 3 paperback

Contents

Acknowledgements

Over the years I have been greatly stimulated by the writings on eighteenth-century Wesleyanism of Henry Rack, John Walsh and Reginald Ward. The centre of this study, however, is the nature and value of religion as such, and here I would hope to add something to what they have said. I have also benefited from the published volumes of the modern edition of *The Works of John Wesley*, of which Frank Baker was for years the editor-in-chief, and from *The Proceedings of the Wesley Historical Society*. I would like to thank for their help the staff at Lambeth Palace Library, where I did research on Archbishop Secker, and the Librarian at Moravian Church House, in Muswell Hill, London, where I worked on John Cennick. I am indebted to staff at the British Library, Bristol University Library, Bristol City Library, the Library at Wesley College, Bristol, and the Library of the Wesley Historical Society at the Westminster Institute of Education, Oxford. My thanks are also due to Peter Forsaith of Methodist Heritage, Ms Noorah al-Gailani of the Museum of Methodism at City Road, London, and Mark Topping of Wesley's Chapel in Bristol for answering my enquiries. My son, Oliver Kent, has given me excellent advice and found me valuable material. I am especially grateful to William Davies, of the Cambridge University Press, for his patience, and to Libby Willis for her meticulous copy-editing.

The Protestant recovery

One of the persistent myths of modern British history is the myth of the so-called evangelical revival. From about 1730 (it is said) a dramatic, divinely inspired return to true Christianity balanced the moral budget of the British people. Lives were changed, society was reformed, and in the longer run the nation was saved from the tempting freedoms of the French Revolution. A Protestant nationalism became the hallmark of the British. The instruments of this divine intervention were John Wesley and his followers, the Wesleyans or Methodists.

In the full-grown version of the myth, the evangelical revival is referred to regularly, not just as an established historical event, but as evidence of the importance of religion in modern history, and even of the importance of a national return to orthodox Christianity in the present day.

What then was Wesleyanism, and what actually happened to give it this role at the centre of a myth, accepted by writers in the United States as well as Britain? Why did it take root in eighteenth-century British society? How did it leave the bitter legacy of the 'Religious Right' in the United States? The answer seems to be that in the 1730s the primary religious impulses of certain social groups, especially in the Church of England, were unsatisfied. The primary religious impulse is to seek some kind of extra-human power, either for personal protection, including the cure of diseases, or for the sake of ecstatic experience, and possibly prophetic guidance. The individual's test of a religious system is how far it can supply this 'supernatural' force. People's primary religious impulses tend to accept a religious system, such as Anglicanism or Roman Catholicism, because it is there, because they knew it when they were children and had their minds tinged with its view of the world. Truth and falsity hardly matter: one is to a degree a product of Buddhism, Christianity, Islam and so on.

Wesleyanism took root and expanded because, in a slowly modernising society, in which until the late 1780s the dominant elites continued to become more tolerant and enlightened in outlook, primary religion also inevitably survived, exercising what we should now call fundamentalist pressure on the existing religious institutions. John Wesley thought that Wesleyanism grew because he was preaching the true gospel, but he succeeded because he responded to the actual religious demands and hopes of his hearers, many of whom thought that religion ought to function as a way of influencing and changing the present, quite apart from what might happen at the future moment when the Second Coming revealed the wrath of God. They wanted a reduction in their personal anxieties, a resolution of their practical problems, and a greater degree of self-approval. This was not a matter of class, and it was certainly not a product of poverty, though at times those who were drawn into Wesleyanism came from groups which had found themselves excluded from the mainstream of eighteenth-century society. Many of those who responded to Wesleyanism were finding their personal existence unbearable. The Wesleys helped them to create space in which they could develop themselves and find new relationships with other people. In effect, Wesley was offering a transformation of personal identity as an antidote to despair or as a cure for circumstances, and it is evident from the start that his approach appealed to numbers of people who were dissatisfied with their personal or social lives.

Historians of eighteenth-century England have usually thought of 'Christianity' and 'religion' as interchangeable terms. The religion of the English was Christianity, or, to put it another way, when the English were being religious they adopted some form of Christianity. This did not imply social unity, because institutionally Christianity had divided. The Church of England had survived the wars of the seventeenth century to become the state church of the Hanoverian dynasty and so the official religion. There was, though, no question of a confessional state – one in which members of the state were automatically members of the Church, and vice versa – because the competing groups of Dissenters and Roman Catholics had also outlasted the time of troubles, and had to be tolerated, however unwillingly, for political reasons. There was no systematic expulsion of either Dissenters or Catholics from the country, on the European model; and in the late seventeenth and early eighteenth century Huguenot refugees were admitted willingly, partly because they were being violently persecuted by the French Catholic state.

In some parts of Europe religious hysteria reached a pitch at which it was respectable to believe that religious cleansing (it could hardly be called 'ethnic') was divinely approved. One can find social reasons for this hysteria, but little evidence that religious leaders opposed such behaviour on religious grounds. When their own group was in the ascendancy they were happy to take advantage of what happened. In England, where the domination of politics by religious forces was dwindling rapidly during the reign of George I, the relationship between the three main religious groups became as much political as religious, and a question of the official position of Anglicanism. Although during the American War of Independence in the 1770s many Anglicans blamed the American secession on the plotting of English Dissenters and became very hostile to them, there was no question of the political leadership expelling English Dissenters to America in order to cleanse the nation; and the deeper social trend (with which the majority of Anglican ministers had no sympathy) was towards giving the Dissenters greater rather than fewer social rights. When the British seized and occupied French Canada, no religious persecution followed, and Lord North's government accepted the legal presence of the French Roman Catholic Church. There were moments when Anglican hostility to British Dissent became oppressive. Thomas Paine (1737–1809), the radical political and religious writer, who had a Quaker background, had to take refuge in America from the 1770s. Joseph Priestley (1733–1804), a liberal Unitarian scientist and political philosopher, also retired there in 1794 as the ruling elites drew together against the revolutionary French. Richard Price (1723–91), a Welsh Dissenting minister who moved gradually towards Unitarianism, was a distinguished moral philosopher who applauded the early stages of the revolution in France, and so found himself the target of Edmund Burke's rhetorical denunciation. But no equivalent of these three Dissenting intellectuals appeared in Hanoverian Wesleyanism.

In Hanoverian England institutionalised religion responded to the social need for ethical norms and for a coherent vision of the world's creation and future. What the apologists asserted was not necessarily religious in itself, but was put forward as truth revealed from heaven. Protestant (and Catholic) Christianity relied on claims – already challenged in the seventeenth century – to the authority of a direct, written self-revelation of the divine as interpreted by various Christian traditions to lay down both the theological system and the ethical patterns by which people would, it was hoped, live their lives. Everyone from the elites to the most wretched shared in personal needs, hopes and anxieties, ranging from a sophisticated dislike of intellectual incoherence to the fear of death as extinction; they also shared, with varying degrees of conviction, the hope that supernatural power might be invoked to ensure one's health, wealth, happiness and so on. Primary religious practices – and it was often more a matter of practice than theory – offered the possibility of harnessing supernatural power.

By the early eighteenth century there could be a wide gap between what ordinary people wanted from religion and what different religious bodies offered, or thought they were offering. There had never been a perfect fit between the intellectual structures of what claimed to be orthodox Christianity and the alternative interests of proliferating local cults, often with a long, varied history. More or less orthodox theologians, men with a strong preference for the linguistic inheritance of Christianity, elaborated ideas of human sin and redemption around the figure of Jesus and the New Testament Epistles, especially those of Paul. Other people were more concerned to obtain supernatural power for a variety of human ends. Evidence of the presence of divine power might be found not only in specific cases of personal and communal 'deliverances' and healings, for example, but also in the form of prophecy, 'spiritual guidance', ecstasies and glossolalia (speaking with tongues). In England, however, official Protestant opinion had become suspicious of claims about divine intervention at any but the most general level, such as the fate of the nation itself, and nursed the fear that religious 'enthusiasm' – the word frequently used to identify the whole bundle of primary religious ideas and practices – could lead to a repetition of seventeenth-century violence and social disruption.

This analysis may help us to see what was happening in eighteenth-century English religion more clearly. One should avoid making too simple a distinction between elite and other ways of being religious, as though the distinction was social – between what the better-educated believed and did, and what was believed and done by the mass of illiterate and often very poor people, in towns as well as in the countryside. 'Popular religion' is a term sometimes used to describe a system of witches, wise women and cunning men, and the charms, curses and fortune-tellings they provided – in which case it seems to denote no more than a particular example of the forms which primary religion has often taken. For example, 'folk religion' is defined as 'a residue of pagan magic and superstition which in some areas exercised a powerful hold over the minds of the common people well into the nineteenth century'.[1] The term is also sometimes used to indicate a set of religious institutions organised by poorer people, for example, working-class people, such as agricultural labourers. This can lead to drawing a thick boundary-line between popular religion and what is regarded as official religion. In the case of the English eighteenth century, however, it would seem a mistake to distinguish sharply within early Wesleyanism (that is, from the 1730s into the 1760s) between one group of followers and another.

Let us distinguish, therefore, a primary level of religious behaviour, when human beings, caught between strong, limitless desires and fears on the one hand, and a conscious lack of power over their situation on the other – and this applies whether one is talking about material or moral needs and ambitions – assert that there may be supernatural powers which can be drawn advantageously into the natural environment; they also suspect the existence of hostile supernatural powers, against which defences must be devised. This fundamental level of religious behaviour should be distinguished from the secondary theologies which develop around it, and which, in the world's religious systems, produce fresh expectations of what being religious means and what effects being religious may have on the individual. Institutionalised theologies are imposed on the primary level of religion and breed sects, denominations, churches, what you will – sources of power in themselves, social and political. But the primary level, with its basic belief in intrusive supernatural power, survives at all times and (and this is frequently forgotten) at all social levels. Belief in an interventionist version of Christianity, for example, is not a product of social position.

We are also too apt to think of religion in terms of theologies, instead of analysing theology in terms of its relation to religion and society. Thus both George Whitefield – a Calvinist, and therefore technically with no use for human free will – and the Wesleys – Arminian, and therefore anxious to preserve a meaning for free will, however abstruse and qualified – took it for granted that what mattered in the activities in which they were taking part was the speculative theology they used to understand and control events. They believed that to satisfy the conditions of salvation one must hold correct views on matters like predestination, an idea which seemed to rule free will out of court, and 'works', a doctrinal description of human effort which limited the possibility of human goodness to the time after conversion. Fierce disagreements broke out at this level, and the competing preachers attributed success to divine approval of their doctrine. They did not suspect that what counted much more than doctrine was the freedom which primary religious aspirations found for at least two generations in the social frameworks which the various Methodist leaders devised.

The Anglicanism in which early eighteenth-century Wesleyanism appeared no longer relied on early modern Roman Catholic methods of harnessing the natural to the supernatural, had dispensed with the Marian theology, and had ceased to direct primary religious activity towards the shrines of local saints; Anglicans had also become deeply critical of the abstract Catholic theology which buttressed the system. This was true of both evangelical and liberal Anglicans.

What got Wesleyan Methodism off the ground in the 1740s was the Wesleys' encounter with and response to the demands of primary religion, a passionate hunger for access to invisible powers, and so for ways of changing the life and prosperity of the adherent. Throughout the early period, as readers of the *Journals* which men like George Whitefield and John Wesley published as a public record of their activities, can see, Wesleyanism hovered at the edge of claiming visible prodigies, miracles in the commonsense meaning of the term, and was often alleged to have done so by Anglican critics. Roman Catholic apologetics had always appealed not only to the miracles described in the Bible and in the history of the early Church, but also to modern, recent evidence of dramatic action by Christ, the Virgin Mary or the saints. Official Protestantism, however, inherited from the sixteenth century a deep suspicion of modern miracles. This was a fundamental theme in the mental processes of the Renaissance as well as of the Reformation, but the liturgical language of Protestantism remained ambiguous, because of its close ties with the language of the Bible, as to how far divine intervention might be expected. There was always the belief, for example, that Providence must prefer the Protestant to the Roman Catholic cause. But these were ecclesiastical or national expectations: it was easier to believe in the providential control of history, in the signs of the times, than to sanction a healing cult in a local Anglican parish church, or approve of the occasional exorcism.[2] On its Hanoverian side the eighteenth-century Protestant recovery was both secular and political, the two facets supplying mutual support for united expansion. The early Wesleyans, however, wanted divine action in everyday life for everyday purposes, whether 'miracle' were the appropriate word or not.

With these distinctions between primary religion and theology in mind, let us look at some examples of eighteenth-century Wesleyan religious behaviour:

On my way to meet Mr Wesley at Perth [in 1769] my mare fell with me, and cut her knees so much, that I was obliged to go to Edinburgh. 'What I do, thou knowest not, but thou shalt know hereafter.' This accident made me visit Dunbar [his birthplace] sixteen or eighteen days earlier than I should have done; where, to my great surprise, I found my mother on her death-bed. I attended her in her last moments; and sincerely hope that I shall meet her in that day when the Lord maketh up his jewels. She had always been a tender and an indulgent parent to me; and her best interests, present and eternal, always lay near my heart. I could not help admiring the hand of Providence that had arrested me on my journey, by the misfortune that befell my mare, that I might once more see my mother before she died. About this time one of the most amiable members of the society died also. She was a sensible and pious woman. I preached a funeral sermon both for her and my mother.[3]

This is a Protestant ex-voto, a characteristic account of how Providence ordered apparently hostile circumstances for the good of the narrator, one of John Wesley's full-time travelling preachers, Thomas Rankin (1738–1810), who was then about thirty years old. The genre did not require illustration, though pictures were sometimes added to make the story more vivid, and the action was attributed directly to Christ or Providence, because there was no question of saintly mediation. In this case the narrator had not even asked for intervention – the divinely controlled accident was an unsolicited favour, an event which showed how Providence, though a little hard on mares, shaped a benevolent world for believers, and watched over the spiritual interests of Rankin and his mother.

The widespread disappearance of images of and prayers to Roman Catholic saints in eighteenth-century England, Scotland and Wales did not mean an absence of effective Protestant intercession, any more than the segregation of the mass in the surviving Roman Catholic subculture meant that the eucharist became unavailable to Protestants. There was no significant spiritual deprivation. The fundamental impulse to ask for supernatural intervention remained unaltered, and found the customary satisfactions. The early Wesleyans cultivated the habit of interpreting selected everyday events as divine action, and as a sign of divine favour, while John Wesley talked about the Last Supper as a 'converting ordinance', which hardly suggests a cult of absent power. Rankin, though Scottish and Presbyterian in origin, became part of the English Wesleyan drive to release the interventionist God from the grip of a moderate Anglican lack of expectation. This also helps to explain his comment on a drunken sea captain, with whom he had sailed between America and England as a young man, that 'he had been truly converted to God; and for years was a burning and shining light; but that fatal opinion, that he could not fall from grace, had been the bane of his spiritual happiness'. If one thinks of 'faith' as 'trust', one might say that two kinds of 'trust' were working here, both equally valid (or invalid), but the Wesleyan characteristically thought that the Calvinist kind of objective trust in predestination had no warrant, and the Calvinist thought that the Wesleyan claim to subjective certainty (assurance) of personal salvation was just as unwarranted. They were not in fact too far apart, because the deep psychological attraction of Calvinism was that the system freed the believer from anxiety about constant ethical failure. Rankin's casual use of biblical quotation is interesting, since the 'burning and shining light' refers to John the Baptist (John 5: 35), the human witness who has to give way to the new, more powerful messenger from heaven.

Rankin's account suggests a mind fed on biblical language. The traditional Christian claim that God had revealed the meaning of the scriptures to the Church (and not, in the last analysis, to the Jews), had made every verse and phrase within a verse in the Jewish Old as well as in the New Testament manipulable by the Christian imagination. In pure theory the true believer's imagination was helped or enlightened by the divine Spirit, but in practice there was no rational limit to what the texts might be made to mean: everything hinged on the style of piety with which they were approached. So Rankin, faced with the unexpected, quoted, careless of incongruity, 'What I do, thou knowest not, but thou shalt know hereafter', a passage which comes from John 13: 7, and is Jesus's answer to Peter's question at the Last Supper, 'Lord, dost thou wash my feet?' In reply, Jesus explains the symbolic intention of the footwashing – that 'you also ought to wash one another's feet' – and at the same time throws out hints that one of the apostles is about to betray him. It was important that Judas's action should be seen to take place within a providential order; Jesus is portrayed as knowing what what was going to happen, and telling his hearers that he would be betrayed.

The context of Rankin's quotation was tragic, but he virtually ignored the Crucifixion narrative and instead drew a parallel between Peter's failure to understand what Jesus was doing and his own initial failure to grasp the significance of the mare's injury. He used the biblical reference to underline what he called the providential nature of the mare's accident. 'I could not help admiring the hand of Providence that had arrested me on my journey, by the misfortune that befell my

mare, that I might once more see my mother before she died.'
This is Providence in Dr Johnson's sense of 'the care of God
over created beings', and the idea is expanded by Rankin with
the further biblical picture of 'that day when the Lord maketh
up his jewels', a reference to Malachi 3: 17, where the Jewish
prophet sees God as promising that at the final judgement the
wicked would be destroyed but that 'unto you that fear my
name the sun of righteousness shall rise with healing in his
wings', a promise which Christian theologians had transferred
to Christians, interpreting the 'sun of righteousness' as Jesus.
God's care for created beings extended to the destruction of
the wicked (including, presumably, the Calvinist sea captain),
but Rankin did not apply that idea directly to his mother,
whom, as he said, he sincerely hoped he would meet among
the jewels. It is worth noting, however, that at a much earlier
point in his narrative he had said that when he was a teenager,
and had lost his father, who been autocratic, 'my mother was
too indulgent and fond of me (as she had never any other son
but myself) and this made her authority but very light over
me – I bless God that I was mercifully preserved from open
wickedness'.[4] Augustine of Hippo casts a long shadow.

   This is very much a preacher's narrative, intended to make
the reader recognise that Rankin's life had been divinely
guided as a series of events in which one could not help admiring the way in which the not altogether invisible hand
of Providence had mercifully preserved him. Others had not
been preserved, and the implication is always that they did not
deserve preservation. He recalled that when the British troops
and American colonists began to fight one another in 1775 he
had told his congregation 'that the sins of Great Britain and
her colonies had long called aloud for vengeance'.[5] This was
traditional pulpit rhetoric, a standard reaction of the professionally religious to the disasters of the nation, any nation.

In practice the war made Rankin a British revival preacher increasingly unwanted in America, because, despite his description of the conflict as a deserved punishment for the sins of the whole community, he fiercely took the side of the Hanoverian regime.

So far we have discussed Rankin in terms of his attitude to religion as the practice of a piety which promotes freedom from anxiety and gives one, in theory at least, a moral superiority to the current state of affairs, because one knows that when things go wrong it is because Providence has moved from judgement to vengeance. Whatever one's sufferings, one is not a subject of that vengeance, but can count on appearing with the jewels at the end of the day. This was not an unusual kind of piety in the eighteenth century. Let us therefore also look at an account which Rankin gave of a service he took in the American Colonies in June 1776, some little distance from Philadelphia, about a year after the battle of Bunkers Hill:

After dinner I observed to brother Shadford that I feared that I should not have strength to preach in the afternoon. A little rest, however, refreshed me, and at four o'clock I went to the chapel again. I preached from Rev 3: 8 'I know thy works'. Towards the close of the sermon, I found an uncommon struggle in my breast, and in the twinkling of an eye my soul was filled with the power and love of God, that I could hardly get out my words. I had scarcely spoken two sentences, while under this amazing influence, before the very house seemed to shake, and all the people were overcome with the presence of the Lord God of Israel. Such a scene my eyes saw, and ears heard, as I never was witness to before . . . Numbers were calling out loud for mercy, and many were mightily praising God their Saviour; while others were in an agony for full redemption in the blood of Jesus. Soon, very soon, my voice was drowned in the pleasing sounds of prayer and praise. Husbands were inviting their wives to go to Heaven with them, and parents calling upon their children to come to the Lord Jesus; and what was peculiarly affecting, I observed in the gallery appropriated to the black people, almost the whole of them upon their knees; some for themselves, and others for their distressed companions . . . As my strength was almost gone, I desired brother Shadford to speak a word to them. He attempted to do so, but was so overcome with the divine presence that he was obliged to sit down; and this was the case, both with him and myself, over and over again. We could only sit still and let the Lord do his own work. For upwards of two hours the mighty outpouring of the Spirit of God continued upon the congregation . . . From the best accounts we could receive afterwards, upwards of fifty were awakened and brought to the knowledge of a pardoning God that day; besides many who were enabled to witness that the blood of Jesus had cleansed them from all sin.[6]

This second account points us to the distinguishing elements of the first two generations of Wesleyanism. In the first passage quoted Rankin described a primary religious attitude which above all helped to diminish anxiety: the value of religious practice was that it brought peace, calmness in the face of life and death. The American example shows us something altogether different, a state of passionate fear and ecstasy in which not only the individual but the whole group felt bound for the moment in a common experience in which they believed they had been possessed by supernatural power. The belief that one could make direct contact as a group with supernatural power in a visibly disorienting way, so that other people could see what was going on, was vitally important.

There are many descriptions of such events, and here is another, more individual, from the account which George Shadford (1739–1816), who came from Lincolnshire, gave of his sister's conversion:

About this time [*c.* 1762], I went to see my sister, near Epworth [in Lincolnshire], to inform her what the Lord had done for my soul. At first when I conversed with her she thought that I was out of my mind; but at length she hearkened to me. She told me a remarkable dream she had some time before, in which she had been warned to lay aside the vain practice of cardplaying, which she had been fond of. After I had returned home, she began to revolve in her mind what I had said; and thought, 'How can my brother have any view to deceive me? What interest can he have in so doing? Certainly my state is worse than I imagine. He sees my danger, and I do not ... ' She therefore could not rest until she came to my father's house; and before she returned, was thoroughly convinced she was a miserable sinner. In a short time I visited her again, and asked her to go to hear Samuel Meggitt preach. She heard him with great satisfaction. Afterwards there was a lovefeast, and she being desirous to stay, at my request, was admitted. As the people were singing a hymn on Christ's coming to judgement, she looked up, and saw all the people singing with a smile upon their countenance. She thought, 'If Christ were to come in judgement now, I shall go to hell, and they will all go to heaven.' Instantly she sunk down as if she were dying, and lay some time before she was able to walk home. She continued praying and waiting upon God for about a fortnight; when one day going to the well to fetch water (like the Samaritan woman at Jacob's well) she found the God of Jacob open to her thirsty soul his love, as a well of water springing up within her unto everlasting life; and as she returned from the well her soul magnified the Lord, and her spirit rejoiced in God her saviour.[7]

The final sentence, which runs together references to Jacob, Jesus, Mary and the Psalms, works in a preaching style to authenticate the woman's experience by identifying it with biblical categories. It is not so much a description as a translation. Like the Samaritan woman, Shadford's sister at first does not recognise the Messiah, but then she feels the springing up of everlasting life in her soul and, like Mary, she is obedient. This actually tells us very little about what may or may not have happened, except for the suggestion that the symbolism of drawing water from her local well played a part. In the whole story of her 'conversion', however, one gets further glimpses of the background. In a familiar formula, the woman has already had a warning dream before her brother comes to her, and the playing cards stand for the society of which pietists disapproved. In the intense communal pressure of the lovefeast (a quarterly meeting of the society, borrowed from the Moravians, at which everybody consumed plain cake and water), her choice seemed to be narrowed to that between heaven and hell, and no doubt she fainted, took time to recover, and found it difficult to walk home. A fortnight later she was convinced, when alone, that God had forgiven her. In effect, she may have done no more than recover her self-approval, shifted from an Anglican to a Wesleyan religious style, and in doing so accepted that she could not leave the social and family group from which she came for another; but at the same time she had, however briefly, felt herself in contact with what she took to be supernatural power. And if the supernatural power existed, it might be turned to for various kinds of assistance on other occasions.

This is a domestic example of how religious power could be used to change oneself. There is a sense, however, in which the resources offered by religion were being used by those who wanted to protest against the surrounding society. There was not much left of the Levellers' mid seventeenth-century hopes of an abrupt eschatological transformation of society into a communal banquet of peace and love, but in the first generation of Wesleyanism (1740–70) the itinerant preachers felt themselves to be at least the intermittent vehicles of an interventionist power with which they could challenge the local social leadership. The dominance of the gentry and clergy had often been attacked in the previous century, and now they frequently reacted violently against the influx of new religious groups into the countryside and small towns. This was dramatically described in the account John Cennick (1718–55) gave of his adventures as a twenty-three-year-old itinerant in Wiltshire in 1741. Cennick had been brought up an Anglican by parents who had originally been members of the Society of Friends, but between 1735 and the early 1740s he moved through Wesleyanism in Whitefield's direction; he started a number of societies in a socially disruptive tour of part of Wiltshire, and ended by taking these groups with him into the Moravian Church, which shared his sympathies with predestination.

Cennick recounts how, on 23 June 1741, Howell Harris, with about twenty-four on horseback, went from Brinkworth to Swindon (both then quite small places).[8] The party was attacked by a mob, which fired guns over their heads, covered them with dust from the highway, and then used an engine to spray them with ditchwater. They returned to Brinkworth. 'This persecution was carried on by Mr Gothard, a leading gentleman of that place, who lent the mob his guns, halbert and engine... and himself sat on horseback the whole time laughing.'[9] The leading gentleman was almost certainly Pleydell Goddard, whose family had held the manor of Swindon since the late sixteenth century, and continued to do so until the middle of the twentieth century. There followed a portent: in a storm 'an oak-tree which stood in a field of Mr Gothard's was split into the finest splinters and scattered all over the field. This seemed to portend somewhat ill.'

When Cennick himself preached at Stratton, a village not far from Swindon, the same mob obtained blood from a butcher to use in the engine, 'because I preach much about the blood of Christ'.

But before I came to Stratton God struck with particular judgements all the authors of this design at once. Mr John and Thomas Violet esqrs, the parson of Stratton and Sylvester Keen a bailiff: all bled at the nose and some at the mouth without ceasing till one of the former fell into dead fits and could not be any more trusted alone. The Minister did not recover until it brought him to the grave, and Sylvester Keen continued to bleed at times at such an extravagant rate that it threw him into a deep decay in which he lingered ten days without having anyone who would come near him because he stunk alive and on March 31 following he died cursing terribly.[10]

Whether these events happened exactly as described does not matter, only that Cennick expected them to be believed. They follow a recognisable pattern, and one of the biblical roots of this kind of story may be found in the account given in Acts of the death of Herod:

> Upon a set day Herod arrayed himself in royal apparel, and sat on the throne, and made an oration unto them. And the people shouted, saying, The voice of a god, and not of a man. And immediately an angel of the Lord smote him, because he gave not God the glory: and he was eaten up of worms and gave up the ghost. But the word of God grew and multiplied.

The divine punishment and terrifying death of the atheist, the blasphemer or the tepidly religious became a staple of eighteenth-century religious literature.

In August 1741 Cennick started a meeting-house in Brinkworth which was to have a long history as a Moravian chapel. On 13 August 1741, when he was preaching at Foxham, another of the small places in the area, another mob, led by a Mr Lee, who seems to have been a farmer, attacked them:

> But after he had done this several of his best horses died, his swine were bitten by a mad dog, and all things made against him till he was ruined and obliged to abscond. He lived in that house which afterwards fell into the Brethren's hands. The others were tried for horse-stealing, and one of them was hanged and another transported.[11]

Rankin's mare was as nothing when compared to this mixed bag of horses and swine, nor is there any obvious sympathy for the wretched human being involved, whose ultimate damnation is more or less taken for granted. The final reversal of fortunes was that the farmer's house fell into the hands of the Moravian Brethren themselves.

What these accounts tell us about the Wesleyan and Moravian mind is that the disappearance of Roman Catholicism from wide areas of eighteenth-century English society

did not make it any more difficult for ordinary people to satisfy the needs of primary religion. In the absence of shrines
devoted to the Virgin Mary and to local saints, people relied for supernatural intervention on direct invocation of the
persons of the Trinity, and especially of the crucified Jesus
or the Holy Spirit. As can be seen above, there was no lack
of apparent results, or any sense of an absence of supernatural power. The contrast between a Catholic and a Protestant
culture, when stated in terms of religious efficacy, has been
much exaggerated; the power of producing a visible effect
might rather be described as equal. One can discount the view
of Maximin Piette that Wesley's career marked the point at
which Protestantism began to recognise the weakness of its
mistaken theology and to turn back in a Catholic direction:
any renewed Protestant vitality could therefore be attributed
to a Catholic source.[12]

The climax of the Wiltshire prodigies was still to come.
Cennick preached at Stratton on 6 September 1741. Fifty on
horseback and fifty on foot went with him from Brinkworth.
Gothard and the Swindon mob came again and dispersed
the meeting. The party withdrew towards Lineham, but 'our
horses were so startled that it was a real mercy we had not
been killed, or killed others that were on foot, for we rode thro
the midst of the people, for our persecutors whipped them
with all their might, while the footpeople to save themselves
rushed into the hedges and hid themselves where they could'.
Cennick's shoulders were black from the blows for three weeks
afterwards. However:

not many days passed, ere, as [Gothard] was riding on the same horse
on which he sat laughing to see us abused at Swindon, a servant of his
was cleaning the guns which had been fouled in firing at us, that letting
one off just as his master rode into the court his horse startled, and by
that means he received some inward hurt either from his saddle or from

his fall which in a little while caused his death, and because he died without a will and his relations did not know who should be his heir, he was left unburied till the stench of his corpse was intolerable . . . He left the world in about a fortnight afterwards raving with pain aged about fifty years.[13]

Pleydell Goddard actually died in 1742, when the estate passed to Ambrose Goddard of Box. One need not assume that Goddard's resistance to Cennick sprang from any religious convictions; his actions expressed the reaction of a closed local community to invasion by 'foreigners'. The *Victoria County History* for Wiltshire notes that throughout the eighteenth century Swindon remained closed to Wesleyanism and Nonconformity in general. The first Nonconformist chapel to be opened there was the Newport Street Congregational chapel of 1804. The divine retribution alleged by Cennick had no other effect as far as one can see.

Rankin's claims that Providence had a hand, so to speak, in the accident to his mare, and that one could feel and (in a sense) see the supernatural forces acting in the Wesleyan meeting – ideas echoed in Shadford's story of his sister's premonitory dream, and of her fainting during the lovefeast, together with John Cennick's passionate belief in the willingness of supernatural power to strike at his opposers – help to throw light on the way in which many educated Anglicans reacted to these fresh examples of primary religion. Few of them would have found Rankin's story of a supernatural power which allegedly lamed a mare in order to bring the Rankins together at a critical moment a cause for admiration, while Cennick's view of Goddard's death would have seemed the survival of an unsophisticated moral sense, rather than evidence of a revival of the proper understanding of Christianity. They would have felt equally negative about George Shadford's description of his sister falling to the floor in a kind of a seizure at the Wesleyan lovefeast, and would not necessarily have agreed that she was reacting to the presence of divine power.

Although Bishop Butler, for example, in his *The Analogy of Religion*,[14] still made the providential pattern of human creation, fall, salvation, and judgement the explanatory theme of human history, his justifying arguments depended on morality, rather than the miraculous. The original revelation of this scheme through scripture and the history of the early Church was certainly (he would have said) authenticated by miracles, but such evidential miracles had ceased to occur; and our later, imperfect human grasp of the divine plan was based on our possession and use of our moral judgement. Butler would have called Rankin an enthusiast, and for Butler the word never quite lost the meaning of someone claiming to be possessed or inspired by a god, a kind of behaviour which should not (he thought) be taken seriously in the eighteenth century. Samuel Johnson defined an enthusiast as 'one who vainly imagines a private revelation', and quoted from John Locke's sceptical criticisms of late seventeenth-century religious pietism in *The Reasonableness of Christianity* (1695). Pietism was a Lutheran reform movement which combined an emphasis on 'rebirth' (the divine creation of a new person in the old sinner) with the idea of setting up local societies of the reborn within the wider Church.

All three Anglicans mentioned above shared the view that it was rash, not to say irrational, to suppose that one could detect evidence of what Butler called the invisible government which Christ at present exercised over his Church. It was generally observed, he said, 'that human creatures are liable to be deceived from enthusiasm in religion, and principles equivalent to enthusiasm in common matters, [here the implied criticism was of secular, political fanaticism] and in both, from negligence'.[15] Religion in its primary sense, a passionate longing for power to transform both the individual and society, had flourished in Europe in the seventeenth century, disastrously. Now, revulsion at what had happened in the past persuaded an intellectual minority, stretching from the deists through liberal Anglicans to commonsense lawyers, that they ought to try to reduce the plausibility of the primary belief in visibly interventionist supernatural forces. Witchcraft, the darkest manifestation of invisible power, and Wesleyanism, which taught men and women to believe they were filled with the Holy Spirit, became equally suspect. This means that while liberal Anglicans in particular also trusted in what seemed to them a benevolent, beautifully designed universe, part of the ground of their faith was that they no longer felt obliged to believe in the kind of detailed supernatural intervention in the details of the common life which fascinated Rankin. How widespread this attitude became can be seen in an essay by the Dissenting philosopher Joseph Priestley, when he commented on David Hume's statement that there was a gloom and melancholy remarkable in all devout people. Priestley replied that what Hume must have seen was 'some miserably low superstition, or wild enthusiasm, things very remote from the calm and sedate, but cheerful spirit of rational devotion'.[16]

What was happening in the early eighteenth century was the partial replacement of an official form of Anglicanism, which had itself developed as a protest against the excesses of a seventeenth-century mixture of religion and politics, by a new expression of primary religion, which eschewed political power and was indifferent to the decline of Dissent, but which also found moderate Anglicanism unresponsive and sought religious forms which took seriously the demand for supernatural empowerment. The early attraction of this new Wesleyan (and initially Anglican) type was that it seemed to be more efficient in calling down supernatural power into the individual's situation. This stress on the individual's immediate satisfaction, in either material or spiritual ways, however modified by theological references, was the point of similarity between the Protestant recovery and the enlightened side of eighteenth-century culture.

This leads us to a further discussion of how primary religion became so prominent in the early eighteenth century. England was then still recovering from the seventeenth-century Civil War and from the long conflicts engendered by Louis XlV's efforts to dominate Europe. European and English Protestantism had survived politically on the field of battle, but was deeply scarred socially and emotionally, both by the rejection of Roman Catholicism and by the conflict between the internal varieties of Protestantism. Primary religious energy had become detached from the main drive of the official forms of Protestantism towards theological self-confidence and social power. In such circumstances one might expect new religious groups to form, less hostile to primary religion, and offering to change the present drastically. Adventist cults had appeared and disappeared throughout the seventeenth century and were visible again at the beginning of the eighteenth. Magic, superstition, prayer, group rituals of various kinds, a search for personal transformation, all interacted to create a lively expectation of the marvellous.

There is much, therefore, to be said against describing what took place on the English religious scene in the first half of the eighteenth century as an evangelical revival, a Christian institutional recovery prompted by the Holy Spirit and involving the recovery of theological preaching of a purer, primitive form of the gospel. This view is part of a conscious, quasi-political desire to provide the evangelicalism of the twenty-first century with a history which may supersede the Catholic and Roman Catholic and Anglo-Catholic versions of the growth and consolidation of the modern Church. Primary religious behaviour does not revive in this technical, theological sense, because, as far as one can see, it does not decline in the first place. At the present time various kinds of fundamentalism, Catholic and Protestant, flourish precisely because they keep close to the primary energies of religion, offering both excitement and power.

The so-called decline of religion is a concept which makes better sense when applied statistically to institutional, professionalised religion. (By professionalised I mean movements which have created a distinct gap between the professional priest or preacher and the laity.) There was, for example, a fall in the number of professional pastors and priests of the traditional Christian type in Europe in the second half of the twentieth century, but that is not necessarily a sign of the decline of religion. The missing professionals have been amply replaced by other kinds of carer, healer, spiritual adviser and wonderworker. Primary religion is liberally provided for, and that gives less scope to groups which concentrate on building up the social and political influence of religious institutions. Primary religion, as a search for ways of bringing divine power into the secular, human condition, seems to be constant: what changes is the relationship between the search and its historical context. There the underlying impulses do seem to gain or lose in self-confidence, in their willingness to be publicly recognised, as well as in their ability to gain public acceptance. In the eighteenth century the Wesleys and their itinerants to some extent restored the freedom of primary religion to be itself in a Protestant context. Examples of healing, prophecy, personal protection, special providences and ecstasy occurred in the Wesleyan societies for a long time and were only very slowly squeezed out in the course of the nineteenth century.

It is in this context that one should approach the problems presented by the growth of eighteenth-century Wesleyanism. English religious life in the eighteenth century did not consist of Christianity, made up of a hegemonic Anglicanism, together with subsidiary groups of Dissenters and Roman Catholics, while on the less well-documented fringes of society there was popular religion, which survived chiefly among agricultural workers and had no importance. As I have already suggested, this description overemphasises the traditional view that an evangelical revival began in the 1730s because a small group of men returned to the primitive faith of Christianity and evoked a fervent response in a largely unconverted population. This was John Wesley's own view of what had happened: for example, he told the Leeds Conference in 1766 that:

in November 1738, two or three persons who desired to flee from the wrath to come, and then seven or eight more, came to me in London and desired me to advise them. I said, 'if you will meet me on Thursday night, I will help you as well as I can'. More and more then desired to meet with them, till they were increased to many hundreds. The case was afterwards the same at Bristol, Kingswood, Newcastle, and many other parts of England, Scotland and Ireland.[17]

In this particular instance Wesley reduced the causation to the work of the Holy Spirit, which impelled people to look for salvation, and to his own role, as being able to tell them what they should do. To these incidents Wesley ascribed his absolute power to appoint when, where and how the societies should meet, and to remove those whose lives showed they had no desire to flee from the wrath to come.

The strong element of primary religion in the first generation of Wesleyanism, from about 1740 to 1770, meant that the steady growth of a new religious organisation had for some time only slight sociopolitical consequences. The early Wesleyan societies were unconcerned about their possible political form or significance. Down to the 1770s the English political elites were involved in extending the overseas empire, cultivating their self-esteem, and increasing their wealth and standing in an aristocratic, hierarchical society. As part of this programme they wanted to maintain the religious arrangements an earlier generation had put in place in the 1690s; these guaranteed the position of Anglicanism as the official form of Christianity, left space for legal but hardly free Dissent, and reduced direct persecution of Roman Catholics to a minimum. This system could, accidentally and at the official level, accommodate the Wesleyan societies, provided they were both Protestant and respectable. The choice remained with the Wesleyans, who were most conscious of occasional ferocious local, often rural, Anglican opposition to their appearance in fresh areas. The country was still recovering from the strains of the previous century and an unpredictable local instability sometimes culminated in violence, in which the agitators seem to have been as likely to label the intruding Wesleyans Roman Catholics as Dissenters. Certainly the grounds for violence were normally that the Wesleyans (or the Moravians in Wiltshire in the 1740s) were not what they claimed to be, and that their real identity threatened a precarious social stability. In 1745, during the Jacobite invasion of England, when choice and loyalty mattered greatly, John Wesley himself, emotionally tied to the Hanoverian succession, openly backed the status quo. Even Jonathan Clark, who contrived a moving fiction of Samuel Johnson as a possible youthful Jacobite sympathiser, would not convince us that Wesley came out for the Young Pretender.[18] Wesley's campaign to push Protestantism deeper into Irish Roman Catholic society could have had immense political repercussions, but years of preaching had little result.[19] Quite apart from the otherness of Ireland, which Wesley suspected but never properly understood, primary religion was already too deeply embedded in Irish Catholicism to need the outlet of Wesleyanism.

By the 1770s the Wesleyan societies of the second generation were beginning to form a denomination, in which some of the emerging body of semi-professional itinerants, who were full-time preachers entirely dependent on John Wesley, were seeking greater official standing. The older group of Anglican Wesleyan leaders (especially Charles Wesley) had at first been deeply affected by their exposure to primary religious energies, and had been carried along by the idea of a self-sustaining, reforming movement, but in their hearts they felt that such a movement had to find a way of coming to rest. They had no enthusiasm for maintaining a separate institution. They wanted what had happened to be accepted by the Church of England authorities and to be gently enfolded within the established system. Even as late as 1775, for example, the not oversophisticated John Fletcher, an Anglican clergyman whose background was Swiss, still thought that Wesleyanism was a movement meant to leaven the established Churches of England and Scotland; he wanted Wesley to approach the Anglican bishops with a request that they ordain selected Wesleyan itinerants, who would bring the societies into close association with the Church of England. What was beginning to work here was a horrified sense of form which found primary religion unbearable. Fletcher, though deeply loyal to Wesley at the level of abstract theology, would not itinerate, but concentrated on his own parish. Fletcher's Methodist Church of England would have defended the Establishment, or an idealised image of it, against Dissent. The new Wesleyan structure he favoured would have had revised Articles and a corrected Liturgy, though the changes proposed did not suggest any theological novelties.

Why any of those concerned should have supposed that the Anglican episcopate would consider plans of this kind is a puzzle, though a certain self-importance, and a desire for improved status in a few cases, probably played a part. To Anglican observers the difference between the Establishment and Wesleyanism was far greater than it seemed either in Fletcher's Shropshire country parish or in Wesley's chapel in the City Road, on the outskirts of the City of London.

There does seem to have been a gradual Wesleyan shift away from contact with primary religion in the second generation of the movement (1770–1800). In the 1770s and early 1780s Wesleyanism had still not settled on its future; the history of local Wesleyan societies suggests that in many cases the principal development came when John Wesley was either very old or dead. What followed differed from what had been the case in the earlier period. Wesley's death in 1791 meant that decisions about continuity could no longer be put off, and that the drive of the itinerants for some kind of ministerial status and authority could no longer be resisted. In the wider society, amid the alarm caused by the French Revolution, moderate evangelical Calvinism was on the brink of an official recognition in the established Church which would enable it to grow into a major ecclesiastical party in the course of the nineteenth century. Wesleyanism made a renewed attempt from the 1790s to throw off anything which would identify the new 'Connexion' with the Dissenting past, and therefore with the turbulent state of the rural and urban working class during and after the French wars.

This did not imply disloyalty to the Wesleyan past. The movement had never responded to the condition of the poor in a political manner. Wesley, like many others, had deplored poverty and encouraged charity; he preached to the disadvantaged, who would listen to him, rather than to the rich, who seldom interested themselves for long in what he said. Eighteenth-century primary religion, whatever its social background, restricted itself politically to a vaguely delineated apocalypticism. There were the French Prophets at the start of the century;[20] there was the wild excitement which transformed the Lisbon earthquake of 1760 into a direct divine threat to London; and there was the wider adventist movement which was stimulated by the French Revolution. Powerful biblical images were briefly charged with primary religious emotion: people were attracted to or horrified by the possibility of a decisive divine intervention which would cancel life's problems and profits at a stroke. But the apocalyptic pictures were aesthetic rather than political; they formed part of the official as well as of the popular stock of Christianity; they illustrated the way that the endgame would go, but they had no lasting political message or effect. At the time of the Lisbon disaster the thought of an apocalypse could still thrill and frighten crowds in a major city like London, but the consequences were no more political than moral. In the twentieth century Orson Welles, in a radio broadcast, had to invoke a Martian invasion to terrify sections of New York's population in a similarly satisfying manner, but New York did not change as a result of the excitement. Such fantasies have too little grip on what people want to flourish for much longer than a firework fiesta.

Indeed, John Wesley's own view of the future was essentially cheerful: in 'The Spread of the Gospel' (1783) and 'The Signs of the Time', a sermon preached as late as 1787, he described Wesleyanism as having started a process of conversion which would spread from heart to heart, from house to house, from town to town, from one kingdom to another, until the world was leavened — leaven being one of the New Testament images of the kingdom of God.[21] This was the closest he came, though he put it in eschatological, and therefore primary, terms, to the benevolent view of creation which appealed widely during the Enlightenment.

The conservative shift of eighteenth-century Wesleyanism stranded a few small, usually urban, Methodist groups which had become attached to radical politics, and were therefore seen in official Wesleyan circles in the 1790s as promoting subversive attitudes. The Wesleyan itinerants did not want Wesleyanism pulled in the direction of Dissent, which was still suffering from the belief of the Anglican elites that Dissent regarded the French Revolution as a natural extension of the democratic and righteous spirit of the American rebellion. From the 1790s onwards any kind of strong external social or political stimulus tended to produce a split in Wesleyanism. This destructive process culminated in the Wesleyan breakdown and institutional divisions of 1849, after which the new United Methodist Free Church and the larger Primitive Methodist Connexion moved in the direction of the radical wing of the Liberal Party, leaving Wesleyan Methodism in the political and religious centre. Neither the Methodist Free Church nor the Wesleyans proper remained closely in touch with what I have called primary religious anxieties and activities, though these may still have been found among the Primitive Methodists in rural areas such as East Anglia as late as the 1880s. In these general terms, Wesleyanism's internal divisions meant that a powerful but somehow impoverished new denomination drifted in the direction of an equally divided Church of England.

2

Early Wesleyanism: 1740–1770

Wesleyanism in the 1740s made contact with the primary religious imagination through the constant assertion that supernatural power was available to the individual believer. Most forms of Christianity talk in this way at times, but it is rarer for this liturgical, evocative language to become the expression of a driving communal conviction. At the beginning of the eighteenth century, after some 200 years of religious troubles, the idea that supernatural power was locally obtainable tended to be carefully controlled. The Wesleys themselves downplayed the notion that the individual's saving faith should include an intense belief in the imminence of a divine Second Coming which would transform visible existence. They preferred to refer to the second advent as an event which would certainly occur, but which was not to be expected in the immediate future; what was available was a more limited, faith-dependent eruption of divine power into the individual or small-group consciousness. The world was not about to change – though for much of the first half of the eighteenth century the Wesleys hoped the Church of England might – but this did not mean that individuals could not find themselves changed, and for a time at least the Wesleys believed they could be changed absolutely. Perfectionism – which in practice was more a state of consciousness, a sense of existing at peace with God without consciously breaking the moral law, than a pattern of behaviour; and which seems effectively to have kept some people in acute anxiety because no one could remain indefinitely in an ecstatic state of consciousness – had few social consequences outside the societies themselves. In comparison with the revolutionary hopes of the seventeenth century this may be called a debased kind of eschatology, but mention of perfect holiness alarmed the eighteenth-century ruling elites, who dismissed such claims (especially when they came from the less-educated part of the population) as conceited, irrational and politically unsound.

The Wesleyan version of 'Christian holiness' did not stir up the political consequences which Anglican writers sometimes feared, because the Wesleyan leaders did not think in such terms, or tolerate indefinitely those who did. Neither John nor Charles Wesley ever went so far as to assert that they themselves had received the divine gift of holiness: they were convinced of divine favour, but not of a total remaking of their personality. Again and again John Wesley records periods when he and whole congregations passionately perceived the immediate presence of the divine, but he translates this in terms of an assurance that his moral mistakes have been forgiven; at the core of the experience his personality remains unshaken, his will is unmoved. This was not the stuff of a primitive, radical rejection of the way in which the social economy worked.

John Wesley's position was intimately connected with 'feeling'. He shared with the early Friends a turn to subjectivity, though he wanted to deny that this was what it was. But one can hardly miss the significance of quotations like this one from one of the official sermons of 1748.[1] Wesley said that the person who had not been 'born of God':

is not sensible of God. He does not feel, he has no inward consciousness of his presence. Hence he has scarce any knowledge of the invisible world, as he has scarce any intercourse with it. Not that it is afar off.

No; he is in the midst of it; it encompasses him round about. Only the natural man discerneth it not; partly because he has not spiritual senses, whereby we can alone discern the things of God; partly because so thick a veil is interposed as he knows not how to penetrate. But when he is born of God, born of the Spirit . . . the Spirit or breath of God is immediately inspired, breathed into the newborn soul . . . and by this new kind of spiritual respiration spiritual life is not only sustained but increased from day to day . . . all the sense of the soul being now awake and capable of discerning spiritual good and evil.[2]

From this point Wesley, pursuing his text (1 John 3: 9, 'Whoever is born of God doth not commit sin'), had to go on to explain in what sense the reborn individual 'doth not commit sin', a task he found doubly difficult because he rejected the Calvinist-Lutheran view which Luther had expressed in the terse comment that the saints can sin and do sin, but equally dared not commit himself to the promise of 'sinless perfection' to which the text seemed to point. He fell back on the defence that 'so long as the one who is born of God keepeth himself (which he is able to do, by the grace of God), the wicked one toucheth him not. But if he keepeth not himself, if he abide not in the faith, he may commit sin even as another man.'[3] This suggested the possibility of a temporary and qualified perfect holiness, whose duration could not be guaranteed, whether one approached the goal by a gradual ascent or by means of instantaneous reception.

Since Wesley did not often find it difficult to argue himself to a conclusion he wanted, even in a case like this, where his problem began because he had accepted the authority of the New Testament as absolute, one may suppose that he wanted this text to be literally true. He could not bear to qualify the passage out of existence, because he needed to believe in the likelihood of radical, personal, supernaturally driven change. He was not appealing to the contemporaneous idea of a moral sense, but talking about an infused moral power, and he was also appealing to these spiritual powers for a shortcut to holiness, the state in which the individual so empowered did not commit sin.

This atmosphere was not that of ethical philosophers such as the Earl of Shaftesbury (1671–1713) and Francis Hutcheson (1694–1746), advocates of the idea of a moral sense, nor was this an ethical attitude with which they sympathised. The shortcut was unavailable in the universe they described, and the feeling that with Wesleyanism one is living in a different culture is increased on turning to the end of this sermon, where Wesley discussed why and how people who had apparently reached a state of holiness could 'backslide', as it was called, into undeniable sin, palpable wrongdoing. His final answer left a disturbing image of God, one which would have a long evangelical history. 'God', said Wesley – and it is important to remember that he believed he was giving the sense of scripture and not inventing his own picture of God – 'does not continue to act upon the soul unless the soul reacts upon God' who:

manifests himself unto us . . . calls us to himself, and shines upon our hearts. But if we do not then love him who first loved us, if we will not harken to his voice . . . his Spirit will not always strive; he will gradually withdraw, and leave us to the darkness of our own hearts . . . he will not continue to breathe into our soul . . . unless our love and prayer and thanksgiving return to him, a sacrifice wherewith he is well pleased.[4]

This sounds very odd, if one takes it to mean more than the pragmatic observation that if one gives up religious habits one ceases to have religious experiences according to the elaborate pattern which the professionals laid down. The theme is picked up in later revivalistic verse: 'Too late, too late will be the cry – Jesus of Nazareth has passed by.'

The passage, given emphasis by coming at the close of the sermon, leaves the impression that God's patience and affection for human beings has a short timespan in terms of eternity, that grace and arbitrariness are reconcilable in the divine economy. One can relate this passage to the letter John wrote to Charles, much later, on 27 June 1766. He described there the continual flatness of his inner religious feelings:

I do not love God. I never did. Therefore I never believed in the Christian sense of the word. Therefore I am only an honest heathen . . . I never had any other proof of the eternal and invisible world than I have now; and that is none at all, unless such as fairly shines from reason's glimmering ray. I have no direct witness. I do not say that I am a child of God, but of anything invisible and eternal.

Nevertheless, he wrote that he was not impelled in his preaching by fear of any kind. 'I have no more fear than love. Or if I have any fear it is not of falling into hell, but of falling into nothing.'[5] No stress should be laid on Wesley's use of the word 'reason', apart from the implication that in his case religious experience had not brought 'spiritual senses' into play; he was appealing to the kind of proofs of God's reality which Hume had already savaged by the 1750s. Both the conclusion of the sermon and the words in the letter have a Calvinist ring about them; they breathe not fatalism but an impression that he has no final freedom, of his being in the hands of a God who might well withdraw his favour and leave him to plunge helplessly into chaos without further hope of rescue. The use of the word 'fear' changes, from the fear of hell, of punishment, which he said he did not have, to a different fear, that of nevertheless not being acceptable. The sentence in his letter reflected Wesley's double conviction, first, that his life as a whole did not deserve condemnation, a view at odds with his fundamental theology; and second, that as he was – and this seems to be a moral judgement, but one not fully worked out – he could not be saved. At times, one suspects, Wesley found himself caught up in the anxiety-machine which he had fastened on his followers, who could hardly appeal to the Calvinistic doctrine of final perseverance, but had to battle on against demons, doubt or depression until hope reconstituted itself or the tormented personality changed and dropped the religious approach to life, or at least this Wesleyan version of it. Several of the Anglican ministers who associated with the Wesleys in the first few years went over to George Whitefield or to the Countess of Huntingdon, or to the Moravians in search of Calvinistic relief from uncertainty.[6] This was the root of eighteenth-century British Calvinism which Wesley could not destroy.

Like many in his own societies Wesley found that he could not feel a comforting inner and divine voice of reassurance, so that, without putting it in clear theological terms, he had logically to rely on election, like the least of Whitefield's congregation. Towards the end of the first Wesleyan wave, on 15 March 1770, Wesley wrote from Arbroath to a Mrs Barton that two things were certain: 'the one, that it is possible to lose even the pure love of God; the other, that it is not necessary, it is not unavoidable – it may be lost, but it may be kept'.[7] He implied that the responsibility lay with Mrs Barton (a follower who had recently received sanctification); that although divine grace was suffcient for her, she must continue to grow, and this meant working even more 'to comfort the feeble-minded, to support the weak, to confirm the wavering, and to recover them that are out of the way', all of which he regarded as evangelical tasks. She, like him, must look for reassurance in the uncertainty of others.

When reading sermons like the one quoted above, the overwhelmingly biblical context of their conception needs to be remembered. Wesley's thoughts were subject to a patchwork of texts from which he could not liberate himself. Although he frequently styled himself 'a man of one book', he nevertheless read many others, interpreting them through the structures of the Bible. Yet he had no positive grasp of a critical approach to the biblical text.

It has been argued that Wesley was a religious empiricist who deliberately drew on the religious experiences of those who surrounded him, and especially on those of Wesleyan women such as Sarah Crosby (*c.* 1729–1804). She had joined the original London society, and moved to Derby in 1761. Wesley allowed her to expound the scriptures and even preach; she travelled widely, and advocated Wesley's perfectionist teaching. Wesley, however, was not a philosophical observer. No one of an empirical temperament would have responded as Wesley did to the claims made for subjective religious excitement made by some of the members of the London society in the early 1760s. George Bell, a former soldier who became a Wesleyan in 1758, and Thomas Maxfield, who had joined Wesley in 1739, both talked in perfectionist language, attempted spiritual healing, and organised a withdrawal from the society of around a fifth of its members in 1763. Bell even declared that the Second Coming would take place on the following 28 February. It was only after Bell's arrest on public order charges that Wesley finally made up his mind and openly attacked him, not for perfectionism but for Adventism.

Yet in the January of 1770 Wesley could still write to Mary Bosanquet (1739–1815), who had been directly involved in the chaos in London, which she left for Leeds in the late 1760s, becoming a de facto preacher there, that it had been salvation from inward sin which above 500 in London had received. 'True they did not (all or most of them) retain it; but they had it as surely as they had pardon. And you and they may receive it again.'[8] Empiricism this was not, but a restless anxiety to believe what others believed at almost any cost.

Wesley's attitude to the possibility of receiving holiness as a direct divine gift remained unaffected by the experience of his followers, and throughout the first wave of Wesleyanism he pressed it on them.

His insistence that even if the Londoners did not retain salvation from inward sin, there could be no doubt that they had felt such a transformation, had its pathos. They doubtless believed what they said, but left Wesley with no ground for the certainty which he asserted. He wrote on the same theme to Mrs Barton in Yorkshire in May 1770. She had recently received sanctification and he wanted to encourage her not to slip back. He told her that 'although many taste of that heavenly gift, deliverance from inbred sin, yet so few, so exceeding few, retain it one year, hardly one in ten, nay one in thirty. Many hundreds in London were made partakers of it within sixteen or eighteen months, but I doubt whether twenty of them are now as holy and happy as they were. And hence others had doubted whether God intended that salvation to be enjoyed long. That many have it for a season, they allow, but are not satisfied that any retain it always. Shall not you for one?'

A genuinely empirical approach to the London events might have led Wesley to ask himself what was the value of this altered state of consciousness, of which he himself clearly had no subjective evidence. Why should one constantly press people to expose themselves to the shocks and disappointment, the infliction of which seemed to be the Spirit's mode of activity? But Wesley remained uninfluenced by the information he had gathered over more than a generation of Wesleyan development, because he interpreted what he saw, or what was reported to him, in terms of a set of biblical texts whose meaning, as far as he grasped it, took precedence over empirical data. A perfectionist subculture stubbornly survived to the end of his life.

Wesley's position as he grew older, surrounded by the rank and file of those who filled his societies, brings to mind what the Victorian painter Edward Burne-Jones, said of his friend William Morris's socialist politics:

when he went into it I thought he would have subdued the ignorant, conceited, mistaken rancour of it all – that he would teach them some humility and give them some sense of obedience . . . I had hopes he would affect them. But never a bit – he did them absolutely no good – they got complete possession of him. All the nice men that went into it were never listened to, only noisy, rancorous ones got the ear of the movement.[9]

Read with an eye for the obvious differences, this goes to the heart of the matter. Wesley was not a man of the new critical culture, nor did he travel all over England collecting and analysing information about the way that religious people behaved. Rather, he was a man with a mission, as Morris was, and he had to accommodate himself, as Morris also did, to those who would join his societies. Both men worked hard to raise the intellectual and moral level of their constituencies. In both cases, however, they had plunged themselves into cultures which they did not fully understand, and whose ways of acting they could modify but not transform. As with Morris, so with Wesley it could be said that although he tried to teach his followers some humility and some sense of obedience, in the end they got possession of him, some of the laity encouraging him to think that he was right about sanctification, and many of the itinerants quietly playing the idea down. Wesley could not establish a critical distance, either from himself, where he needed to make moral judgements instead of fussing about states of feeling, or from the more assertive members of his movement, whose states of mind – especially in the case of the women – were more closed to him than he realised or would have liked to face. He paid the penalty for letting himself be detached from the intellectual preoccupations of his age, and his attitude to claims about the spiritual life ceased to be empirical, because he had adopted precritical standards.

As far as the 'confessional' letter which John wrote to Charles Wesley is concerned, one should beware of reading it in too modern a context, of taking it for granted that Wesley was writing in the style of Kierkegaard, or suddenly revealing a previously concealed scepticism. Martin Schmidt, for example, clamed that 'this was a thoroughly modern feeling which seized his soul. The traditional concepts had lost their potency, and nihilism was beginning to make itself felt in the form of a horror of complete emptiness and absurdity.'[10] Schmidt is very perceptive on Wesley's character, but here I must disagree. Wesley was admitting that he had not found sanctifying faith, and even that he rarely became conscious of the presence of the divine Spirit, though his accounts of Methodist society meetings in the *Journal* would become suspect if one took this statement as exact. What he was expressing, for all that he denied that he was overcome by fear, was a deep dread of an inscrutable divine power, which might be satisfied, even well pleased, with a 'sacrifice of praise and thanksgiving', but which could choose not to be pleased and could, so to speak, walk away, abandoning the human soul not to hell (because hell was a place for the negative, or deliberate sinner, and for active punishment) but to a special limbo reserved for rejected Arminians. Their epitaph might be rendered: they danced, but they did not please. Schmidt argued that: '[Wesley] trusted God not only with a childlike faith in providence, but with all the tenacity of a mature man who was clear in his own mind as to what he was doing and what he was risking, but who in his decisions and actions knew himself to be only a tool in the firm grasp of him who had laid his hand upon him.'[11] Rather, what Wesley relied on was the effect of his preaching, which still led in the 1760s to great excitement and conversion. But the Calvinist flavour remains: nothing guarantees the final vision of God.

The sermons on holiness appeared in 1748 and Wesley made no substantial alterations later on, though in reply to criticism, both Nonconformist and Anglican, he issued supplementary, but not radically changed, accounts of his teaching on holiness. From the later 1760s he tried to set his 'Connexion' on a permanent footing, which required a behavioural shift towards respectability, some playing down of the ecstasy of the past, and perhaps a kinder, less threatening stress – understandable in the light of his letter to his brother – on the possibility of people cooperating with God in finding personal holiness. But the letters from 1770 quoted previously show that as a spiritual director – which is what his role in the societies became as time went on – he still insisted on the need to 'press forward to perfection'.

In the decisive decade between 1738 and 1750, and again in the Wesleyan troubles which marked the period of the Seven Years War (1756–1763), together with the campaign of holiness testimonies which Wesley ran through the *Arminian Magazine* from its first publication in 1778, Gordon Rupp saw support for the image of Wesley as an 'apostolic man' with a genuinely enlightened interest in religious phenomena.[12] Professor Rupp quoted one of Wesley's early clerical corrspondents, 'John Smith', as saying ironically that Wesley felt called to 'the apostolate of England'; Rupp commented that a hundred years later men would think that something rather like that had been going on. Wesley did think of himself, not precisely as apostolic, but as a man entrusted with a national mission, who dared not stop his revolving itinerancy. The Wesleyans themselves came to treat him as what we might now call a charismatic figure.

Whether the quality of his understanding of his mission was apostolic is another question. It is interesting to compare him with French intellectuals of the period who wrote and campaigned in the field of religion. He never analysed the religious reactions of his followers with the subtlety with which the materialist philosopher Denis Diderot, for instance, analysed the psychology of religious asceticism and female suffering in his novel *La Religeuse*, which was written in the 1760s, although not published until 1796, after his death. And when Jean-Jacques Rousseau answered the scepticism of the Parisian intellectuals, it was with a Shaftesbury-like subjective invocation of the goodness of the human heart and with an appeal to the religious inspiration of landscape which had no parallel in Wesley's writing: he had no taste for nature-mysticism. There are more ways than one of acting out an apostolate, and Rousseau influenced the piety of the nineteenth-century European bourgeoisie more deeply than Wesleyanism did.

Wesley held the mistaken view that moral decisions were simple; that what one needed, given that Jesus had laid down the essential moral law, was a supernatural transformation of the will. In practice, Wesleyan holiness meant altered states of consciousness, brief in themselves, and with no lasting effect on the will or personality. Wesley accepted the definition of holiness which demanded loving God with all one's heart and mind and soul and one's neighbour as oneself. But neither the presence of the Spirit nor the pursuit of love helped him and his followers to a clearer understanding of their own and other people's motives. After the first wave of Wesleyanism the societies gradually lost their appetite for ecstatic experience, because the members were beginning to feel themselves in control of their social and personal circumstances. Wesley recognised and deplored this shift from dependence to independence.

As far as John Wesley is concerned, V. H. H. Green's penetrating description of his old age remains valid:

Ultimately, like so many of the Christian saints, John Wesley was self-regarding . . . His life was built around his own experience, an experience glazed and insulated from the outside world by his confidence in God and in himself. Completely selfless and yet intensely egoistic, he had come to identify himself with his own creation . . . The diaries [Wesley's *Journals*] form one of the most consistently complacent documents ever written, and the more religious he became the more free from human frailty he appeared to be. Apart from the period of his early life his entries are almost devoid of doubt and self-criticism. Self-satisfied and self-regarding, yet by his unstinted selflessness he made himself wondrously loved. Nothing could justify the wild attacks of the neo-Calvinists and the writers in the *Gospel Magazine* but their fury, like his wife's rages, may have been provoked by his untouchability, the hard centre of his personality.[13]

Dr Green's summary underlines the weakness of Wesley's reliance on the sources and results of primary religion, his frequent inability to distinguish between moral and emotional energy. This weakness did not develop in old age, but had dogged him throughout his life. The comparatively slow growth of the societies of the first wave reflected this.

Mirroring the slow development of the early Wesleyan societies, there was no wide English religious movement outside them in the 1740s and 1750s: there was, for example, little Dissenting expansion. Neither the Baptists nor the varieties of Independency and Presbyterianism recovered much in the first half of the eighteenth century. Even the Moravians, who were swept by powerful religious emotions in the 1740s, did not attempt to expand after 1750, and their settlements – self-sufficient, pietist villages – had less influence than they deserved. This happened partly because Wesley – although he had, in 1738, under Moravian auspices, first felt what might be called a physical sensation of forgiveness – soon ceased to forgive his mentors. He criticised them endlessly and bitterly, both for their Calvinist tendencies and for their 'stillness', the habit of waiting until one was certain of a divine prompting before passing on to action. Baptist growth always suffered when it reached that large section of the population which preferred infant baptism, a sacrament long established as a rite of passage.

A Protestant institutional renewal of confidence, to which the Methodists contributed, did take place, but the explanation of what happened lies largely at a secular level. Protestantism as a world movement recovered to a remarkable extent from its hard-pressed situation in the 1690s, when the Counter-Reformation states still seemed to have it in their power to put an end to serious opposition. The change in Protestant fortunes was military and political rather than religious. Prussia, firmly under the control of the Hohenzollern family, became an aggressive Protestant state, bent on reorganising Germany politically to its own material advantage, and on reducing the power of the Roman Catholic Habsburgs to the south-east and of Catholic France to the west. Hanoverian England, with its German Protestant royal family, solidly supported the Prussians. A decline in political and military power affected European Roman Catholicism, which began to look soft-centred by the 1740s, though it was only during the French Revolution that the Vatican discovered how weak its grasp on European culture and society had become, and how deep ran civil resentment against the political power and form of its institutions. Women would rescue the Roman Catholicism which men had mismanaged, but Europe would not revert completely to the ancien regime.

In England Anglicanism slowly strengthened its grip on the political community under the first two Georges, and this meant that Protestantism gradually identified itself with a new

British nationalism.[14] For the time being Roman Catholicism in England could survive and slightly increase, but it could not prosper. Neither the Stuart dynasty nor the Roman Catholic Church restored its former position in England – a political fact which had become obvious by 1745, when the new Wesleyan societies rejected the Jacobite invasion. Britain gave Protestant culture a potentially vast new powerhouse by the completion of the conquest of North America at the expense of the French, and here, unlike Ireland and Scotland, the American provinces proved fertile ground for the Wesleyan itinerants. In turn the political and economic strength of Britain and the new United States would rapidly enable Protestant missionary societies, including the new Wesleyan Methodist Missionary Society, officially founded in 1818, to compete with Catholic missionary orders in much of the world outside Europe. One of the stranger examples of competition was the Wesleyan campaign to establish societies in France: this was no more successful than the earlier campaign in Catholic Ireland.

The Protestant crisis ended by 1815, and it is evident that the Protestant churches had benefited as much from economic, military and political change as they did from the First and Second Great Awakenings in America and from the spread of Wesleyanism in Britain itself.[15] George Whitefield (1714–70) visited the American Colonies seven times, going particularly to New England. The First Awakening certainly reinforced Protestantism as the dominant form of American religion; it ran parallel with the first Wesleyan generation from the 1740s to the 1770s, but the overall effect was divisively disastrous.

Whitefield encouraged a predominantly Calvinist tone, hostile to the Wesleyan holiness movement but equally concerned to produce ecstatic conversion experiences. The revivals split both the Baptists and the Presbyterians, because of the number of American ministers who were open to the influence of new philosophical ideas: Harvard, after all, had been founded in the seventeenth century. As in England, the intelligentsia, small though it was, urban, and not yet powerful, was questioning the orthodox Christian account of a virtuous life, of how one should behave if one wanted to become a good man or woman. At the same time American intellectuals moved steadily towards the radical view that the modern state had its own foundation, independent of organised religion, in a concept of the freedom of the mind which guaranteed citizens equality whatever their religious allegiance or lack of one. The federal constitution accepted the supremacy of divine justice, but gave no specific Church the authority to define either justice or the structure of American citizenship. This amounted to a dissent from Dissent itself, and was in line with David Hume's opinion that there was no method of reasoning more common, nor more blamable, 'than in public debates to endeavour to refute any hypothesis by a pretext of its dangerous consequences to religion and morality'.[16] Wesleyan preachers came into the picture about 1760, but they made no attempt to place the new Wesleyan societies in subjection to the Anglican hierarchy in the Colonies. The itinerants sent from England sometimes longed, as we have seen, to take the dynastic side in the American struggle, but they knew that the majority of American Wesleyans wanted separation from the Anglican establishments.

The movement played a much larger role in the Second Awakening, which remains even more controversial than the First, and lasted from about 1800 to the 1840s.[17] Both revivals depended heavily on acting as channels for primary religious energies, and Wesleyan holiness preaching featured prominently after 1800. These revivals did not revive or reform Anglicanism: they often gave a Wesleyan character to Northern Irish and German Protestants who had emigrated to

America, and who had no interest in an Americanised Church of England. By the 1770s in England itself even the monarchical party of Lord North no longer thought that religious uniformity was necessary to national identity. There is no need to suggest a temporary loss of nerve on the part of the Anglican elites, whether in England or in America, as Jonathan Clark has done.[18] In neither country was there a confessional state, one in which membership of the Church automatically defined one as a subject of the state, and being a subject equally defined one as owing a duty to the established Church.

If one goes back to the 1740s, then, Wesleyanism may be interpreted not as a revival of primitive Christianity (one of Wesley's favourite descriptions) but as an attempt to redefine Anglicanism, and even to restore Anglican clerical claims to authority over the laity. Wesleyan evangelism did not stop at the conversion of the individual, but required the bonding together of the converts, first into small classes, some for men and some for women, with leaders drawn from their members; and second into societies of which the final oversight remained in the hands of the Wesleys and their handful of clerical helpers. Ideally these societies might have become the parish, and then a kind of social revolution would have taken place, but this was only possible where the incumbent sympathized with the Wesleyans, a situation Wesley made less likely by his steady attacks on Anglican moderate Calvinists, as well as on Dissenters and Moravians. The idea of reforming the Church of England did not have a wide social appeal, if such a reform implied the strengthening of the claims of the local parish to play a decisive role in defining, governing, and in some cases even policing society. (Such a struggle for control lay at the root of the eighteenth century's inability to organise effective poor relief on a parochial basis.) This was not so much a lack of faith as a pragmatic lack of faith in the value of

faith. Those who flowed naturally into the new Wesleyan societies were less obsessed with professional, clerical direction
than with primary religious impulses, which responded less
freely to the idea of salvation from hell than to the guarantee
of survival and happiness in the here and now.[19]

So if one asks the familiar question – why did the Wesleyan
movement succeed in the 1740s? – one encounters the traditional response that the country had become corrupted by
deism, immorality and social insubordination, against all of
which the evangelical revival came as a triumphant reaction.
What is really fascinating about this explanation is not only
that as late as the 1820s in north Somerset a parish priest like
John Skinner and his bishop (George Law, of Bath and Wells)
were still repeating the same list of the forces that had destroyed the cohesion of society, but that they now added to it
as a clincher the evangelical passion with which both Primitive
Methodist local preachers and evangelical Anglican parsons
asserted their certainty that they knew they had been saved.
Neither education nor ignorance, thought Law and Skinner,
who were both High Churchmen, justified this willingness to
contradict the teaching of the clergy and the bishops.[20]

Nevertheless, one can still quote a history textbook of the
1990s which states that 'what the hungry and lost sheep needed
was a message of salvation, rooted in hope and directed at
the heart. They might never have received that message, and
indeed Christianity might conceivably have lost its hold on the
bulk of English men and women entirely by the end of the eighteenth century, but for the beginning, in the 1730s, of what we
now know as the Evangelical Revival.'[21] This view should
be balanced against a version of eighteenth-century religious
history which starts from the assumption that the many drives
which constantly go to produce religious behaviour would
have operated in eighteenth-century England even if the

'revival' had not taken place. Neither poverty nor emotional crises were about to disappear, and neither medicine as it was nor miracle as it might have been freed the population from the knowledge of death.

Moreover, English radical philosophy in the tradition of John Locke (1632–1704), Samuel Clarke (1675–1729), Shaftesbury and Hutcheson offered no direct threat to eighteenth-century primary religion, as distinct from Christian theology. 'Deism' has become too uncertain a term over the years to be very useful: radicalism is more inclusive. It is true that these writers dismissed any simple idea of a divine personality willing to intervene in the affairs and emotions of individuals. They reacted against any institutionalised theological system which might generate or justify social or political passion, a reaction against the perceived results of Christianity in the bitter wars of the seventeenth century. This did not mean there were grounds for claiming that theological radicalism corrupted society: to encourage a more sensitive, self-conscious attitude to morality, to advocate scepticism about witchcraft, to protest against the theological dogmatism of the Churches – none of this struck at the root of civilised behaviour.

In any case, these philosophers' views did not touch the majority of ordinary people in the first half of the eighteenth century. The world in which the Wesleyans flourished believed that criticism of Christianity was being refuted by a visible display of divine power in everyday life. At the same time the settling down of an officially Protestant culture meant that most people no longer turned to local Roman Catholic saints to ask for divine intervention, and this was important, because the well-known images of these men and women had in the past made it easier for many people to grasp the notion of appealing to a quasi-human intermediary with special powers of intercession qualified to bring help. It is not fanciful to see in the Wesleys and Whitefield in the early part of their careers men who were, unconsciously, playing something similar to the role of the saint who served his faithful petitioners. When the early nineteenth-century Wesleyan painter Marshall Claxton (1813–81) painted a picture of *The Mobbing of John Wesley at Wednesbury*, an event of the 1740s, the mob might be described as Hogarthian but Wesley, pale, calm and uplifted, seems to come from another world. Claxton's version of what had become myth by the 1840s still hinted at the original relationship between the leader and the led.

The paradox of the origins of early Welseyanism lies in the role which primary religion played. Writing about Ludwig Feuerbach, the nineteenth-century German philosopher of religion who emphasised the creative part played by the popular imagination in the primitive shaping of Christianity, the American scholar Van A. Harvey, observed:

> the ordinary believer wants a deliverer, a superhuman power which can set aside and overcome the inexorability of necessity and fate, that can save and redeem. The ordinary believer is not interested in abstract beliefs and doctrines, except in so far as these articulate the faith that the gods are committed to the well-being of the creature. Consequently, the interpreter of religion must acknowledge that petitionary prayer and worship, belief in miracles and deliverance from suffering and death are the core of religion even if theologians are normally embarrassed by this naive piety.[22]

The Moravians, Wesleyans, Whitefieldites and other groups which prospered with the return of Protestant political self-confidence tolerated the kind of demand which Harvey describes, and happily absorbed into their experience what both moderate Anglicans and radical intellectuals regarded as a mixture of superstition and delusion.

For example, when John Wesley preached at Spen, eight miles south-west of Newcastle upon Tyne, on 17 November

1743, on the text 'Christ Jesus our wisdom, righteousness, sanctification and redemption', he recorded that he had seldom seen an audience so greatly moved since the time of his first preaching at Bristol.

Men, women and children wept, and groaned, and trembled exceedingly. Many could not contain themselves in those bounds but cried with a loud and bitter cry. It was the same at the meeting of the society, and likewise in the morning, while I was showing the happiness of those 'whose iniquities are forgiven, and whose sin is covered' (Romans 1: 7). I afterwards spoke with twelve or fourteen of them severally, and found good ground to believe that God had given them to 'taste of the good word and of the powers of the world to come'.[23]

A subculture of tears and cries and of 'the powers of the world to come': this, not abstract beliefs and doctrines, in an atmosphere radically unlike that of the parish church, reflects not only Harvey's comment, but Feuerbach's understanding of the power of the small community to generate its own religious images, rites and music.

Scholars sometimes argue that Wesleyanism began as part of the gradual expansion of pietist influence from the late seventeenth century into the 1730s throughout the Protestant world.[24] Professional historians have become noticeably cautious about interpreting, as distinct from recording, eighteenth-century religious material. They hesitate to go beyond reporting the pietist explanations of the spread of new religious movements given at the time, according to which what were called revivals were the results of 'extraordinary outpourings of the Spirit', for which God rather than man took the responsibility. In later life John Wesley was fond of recalling how, years before, 'two young men without a name, without friends, without either power or fortune, set out from College with principles totally different from those of the common people, to oppose all the world, learned and unlearned'.[25]

This was a pardonably romantic view of the past. It is evident from what we have already said that Wesley's religious principles did not differ totally from those of the common people. The reverse was also true, and played a large part in his success. As for the 'world', he had a fluctuating relationship with the beau monde or 'society', where early Methodism sometimes featured as a fashionable subject of the season, though the greater outcast was George Whitefield, who remained the prime symbol of Methodism until his death in 1770. Whitefield was the target of a succession of stage satires, the best known of which – *The Minor*, by Samuel Foote – was first put on the London stage as late as 1760.[26] As for the 'learned', Wesley faced personal episcopal criticism almost from the start, but the serious public attacks come later: George Lavington (1684–1762), the bishop of Exeter, published *The Enthusiasm of the Methodists and the Papists Compared* in 1749–51, and William Warburton (1698–1779) published *The Doctrine of Grace*, which was directly aimed at the Wesleyan cult of the Holy Spirit, as late as 1762.

Intellectual opponents of Christianity itself concentrated their attacks on the doctrine of the Trinity or the authority of the text of the Bible. Wesley did not 'oppose all the world' nor was he entirely without friends: he exaggerated his isolation when he agreed to go to Bristol in 1740, where George Whitefield had been before him, but he could claim that in the field of the 'learned' he had had almost from the beginning to resist clerical attack from all denominations. On the other hand, he used this opposition to justify his own divisive tactics, insisting on the importance of loyalty to himself and on the moral insufficiency of the theology of his competitors.

It is easy to underrate the value of the flexibility of the Church of England, which, for all the talk of opposition, never formally expelled the Wesleyans, and tolerated the virtual institutionalisation of the evangelicals Anglican towards the end of the century. Anglicanism could not be accurately defined in terms of either the High Church or the evangelical prescriptions, and scepticism about these distinctions was laying the foundations of Anglican liberalism in its turn. There had been an Anglican war of labels ever since the sixteenth century. The Church of England had been invented to save the country from the external authority and absolutist opinions of Rome, and this remained its most useful function.

The Anglican authorities could have legitimised Wesleyan activities, but two problems prevented this. First, in the vital early years official recognition could have come about only on Wesley's terms; and second, the episcopate did not accept Wesley, then or later, as entitled to lay down the nature of Anglican theology, either on justification or on sanctification, or as qualified to make dismissive statements about the state of the souls of swathes of the Anglican clergy. Wesleyan preaching attacked the individual directly and aimed at changing the hearer's consciousness. *You* are a sinner, you cannot change yourself into the righteous person whom God alone will admit to heaven. *You* need divine forgiveness: without it you are damned. (Persistent attempts to argue that itinerant preaching did not depend heavily on the threat of damnation are unconvincing.) *You* can have forgiveness now, through faith in the sacrificial death of Jesus Christ. And you can know that *you* have been forgiven, because the Holy Spirit will tell *you* so. However briefly, *you* will be filled with ecstasy.

Wesley's tactics went too far for Anglican opinion. His willingness to say that anyone was personally free at this moment to respond to the offer of justification contradicted the widely held assumption that theologically the sinner had no choice, being either divinely chosen or not chosen. Unintentionally, Wesley anticipated the general direction in which

Protestantism would go, towards greater reliance on the individual's freedom to judge, to choose and to act. The combined stress on freedom to choose and freedom to become ecstatically certain that one had received what one had chosen in the moment of faith offended Anglican ideas not only of order and decorum, but also of the place of humility in religion. This reticence did not necessarily arise from coldheartedness – the claim that 'heart religion' flourished only in evangelical circles should not be taken too seriously – nor from the rational piety of the Hanoverian 'civic religion', which concentrated on raising the ethical tone of all ranks of society, though this could have an equal sense of human limitation, of the need for silence as much as for speech.[27] The same feeling for individual freedom which led Wesley towards excess led many Anglicans in a much more private direction.

   This point is put from another direction by John Brewer in his article 'The most polite age and the most vicious':[28]

The eighteenth-century phenomenon . . . is usually understood in the English case as an attempt by politically moderate (but usually Whig) aristocrats and gentlemen, liberal and latitudinarian clergy, and prosperous Dissenting/Nonconformist interests to create a polite culture. This culture was characterized by its proponents as moderate and reasonable. Usually Christian (though it eschewed clerical controversy and theological dispute as the divisive dogmas of the academy and priesthood), it invariably rejected the court as the focus of culture, even though, in some of its manifestations, it was committed to aristocratic leadership. Its object . . . was to constitute and instruct a public – a body of arbiters of taste, morality and policy – and the means by which this goal was to be achieved was through the art of politeness. Politeness was construed both as a technique and as an end. Its aim was to shape and unify a disinterested, reasonable and discriminating public, without which there could be neither good taste nor moral virtue.

   Here one has to emphasise that the setting up of a polite culture was not a matter of building a mannered facade to hide the absence of serious religious feelings. James Boswell, for example, spent his life in search of a close, male-club culture in which he could share with others such as Samuel Johnson and Thomas Barnard (Anglican bishop of Killaloe and Kilfenora in Ireland) his personal moral difficulties, his theological uncertainty and the unhappiness, constantly expressed in religious forms, which his depressive temperament caused him. In a muddle of sex, drink, doubt and dread of damnation, Boswell made this polite society with its conventions the environment in which, not unlike the Wesleyans, he looked for an epiphany. Unlike the Wesleyans, he did not find one.

Few forms of Anglicanism, however, could accept the vision of a Christian life which sought climactic, communal ecstasy. Integral to the first-wave experience was the Wesleyan discovery of the congregational singing which fed on the hymns written by Charles Wesley, a prolific versifier of doctrine and of biblical texts (and, at a later stage, of the part played by Providence in the American War of Independence). In 1700 there had not been much hymnsinging in parish churches. Organs of any kind remained rare until the end of the century. Now, however, parish choirs formed, and rapidly became popular on a national level. The singers had a special pew and from about 1740 a band of two to six wind instruments was common. As Nicholas Temperley explained: 'the most characteristic form for these choirs was the "fuging tune" . . . more than six hundred examples were printed in England before 1800. It was a strophic setting of a metrical psalm . . . the congregation could not join in or even, in many cases, understand the words being sung . . . the tunes . . . had the vitality and freshness also characteristic of the New England composers of the Billings school.'[29] There were also parochial anthems, hundreds of which were written for parish choirs, a further sign of the vitality of eighteenth-century Anglicanism.

In about 1754 John Wesley, determined to protect his societies from a musical culture which he regarded as preventing
effective religious worship, arranged for the publication of
a collection of tunes under the title *Harmonia Sacra*. In the
Preface to a second version, *Select Hymns with Tunes Annext*
(1761), he commented modestly: 'I believe all unprejudiced
persons who understand music allow that it [the collection]
exceeds beyond all degrees of comparison anything of the
kind which has appeared in England before.' He attacked the
'masters of music' on the same grounds as Temperley, that
their arrangements buried the tunes, handed the service over
to the choir, and made it impossible for the congregation to
sing the words.

He went much further in 1779, in a brief essay called
'Thoughts on the Power of Music', asserting that 'our composers do not aim at moving the passions . . . what has counterpoint to do with the passions?' He contrasted this state of
affairs with the music of the classical Greeks, which had, he
claimed, all the emotional power denied to those whose taste
had been corrupted 'by attending to counterpoint and complicated music'. No sensible person, he said, would deny the
greater effectiveness of ancient music, 'for it would be denying the faith of all history', that is, the authority of all classical
texts, including the Bible.[30] The style of argument, the reliance
on what had so long possessed authority, the habitual disre-
gard for the growing practice of historical criticism, vividly
illustrated his intellectual limitations as a leader, his lack of
sympathy for anything which he had not been taught when he
was young, the difficulties confronting any attempt to present
him as influenced by the Enlightenment. But his anxiety, not
just to make the words and teaching of the hymns accessible,
but also to excite the passions of his congregations, should be
noted. This was more than a Protestant devotion to the Word;

here was a direct and at times highly successful appeal to the feelings.

In the following year, 1780, Wesley published the *Collection of Hymns for the People called Methodists*. Most of the more significant hymns had been written by his brother Charles in the years of the first wave. The hymnbook expounded the Wesleyan theory of holiness at length. Hymn 344, for example, written in 1742, included the verse:

> Lord, if I on Thee believe,
> The second gift impart;
> With the indwelling Spirit give
> A new, a contrite heart.

It culminated in the verses:

> Grant me now the bliss to feel
> Of those that are in Thee;
> Son of God, Thyself reveal,
> Engrave Thy name on me.
>
> As in heaven be here adored,
> And let me now the promise prove,
> Help me Saviour, speak the word,
> And perfect me in love.[31]

Hymn 388, which was written in 1749, ends with the prayer:

> Hasten, Lord, the perfect day,
> Let thy every servant say,
> I have now obtained the power,
> Born of God, to sin no more.[32]

The modern editors of the 1780 book comment: 'does the "perfect day" really refer to the second coming, or is it not more likely that Wesley has the "second blessing" in mind, leading to the affirmation, "I have now obtained the power"?[33] They add that this affirmation goes beyond what is written in 1 John 3: 9, but Wesley himself would not, I think, have agreed with this conclusion, because he took the point of the New Testament saying at its face value, as meaning 'He that is born of God cannot sin.' In Wesley's mind this meant that one could be born again *now*, and so enabled to sin no more: one did not need to wait for the experience of perfection either until death or until the Second Coming. Charles Wesley's plea for an immediate personal transformation is perfectly clear, and its consequences are in fact made explicit in the following hymn, 389, which also dates from 1749, so that the connection between the two is established:

> When Thou the work of faith hast wrought,
> I here shall in thine image shine,
> Nor sin in deed, or word, or thought:
> Let men exclaim and fiends repine,
> They cannot break the firm decree,
> All things are possible to me.

Charles Wesley's role in the first wave of Wesleyanism as preacher and hymnwriter has been played down unduly. One is bound, however, to question the very large number of hymns which he wrote on the doctrine of holiness, and ask whether these do not repeatedly offer more than he experienced himself or perhaps believed. He frequently criticised his brother's willingness to credit people who claimed to have received the second blessing, but he also wrote as though all that was needed for its reception was faith, and that no major problem existed about what followed afterwards. The fact that the Wesleyans came to use their hymnbook as a prayerbook meant that they immersed themselves in these questionable devotional attitudes. Charles himself seems to have been not much worried about the effects of what he wrote.

H. D. Rack, in his excellent biography of John Wesley, argued that Wesley's ideas and language seemed closer to

Roman Catholic than to Protestant spirituality. He added that 'the most obvious Protestant precedent in George Fox and the Quakers is unlikely to have influenced him'.[34] What Wesley admired in the Roman Catholic writers whom he included in his multivolume *Christian Library* was the singleminded self-sacrifice with which they pursued their concept of holiness.[35] As for early Quaker teaching about holiness, Rack's suggestion looks true in the form in which it is put, because Wesley shared the Anglican clergy's social and political antipathy towards all forms of Dissent, and there is no evidence that he had been personally impressed by reading what George Fox had written about ecstatic experience of the divine Spirit. Nevertheless, in the first wave of Wesleyanism he attracted many Friends, who must have interpreted what he taught in the light of their own past.

In these matters too much attention can be paid to the Wesleys themselves. Wesleyanism was a communal creation. The seventeenth-century Friends spread widely, partly because they provided a channel for the social mood which would have made England more like a republic than a dynastic possession. But above all the Friends practised a democracy of religion, and an equality between the sexes in being moved by the Spirit, keeping alive ideas which affected the expectations and behaviour of many of the people who joined the Wesleyan societies in the 1740s. Wesley had an ambiguous attitude to the early Friends' way of taking freedom for granted, and the advance of Wesleyanism ran parallel to the decline of the Friends, partly because Wesley himself insisted on a more authoritarian system.

A chastened, smaller Quaker movement emerged from the wreckage of seventeenth-century radicalism, led by men who had gone into local business, banking, brewing and other small industries with a big future. They specialised in a sophisticated, high-minded style of critical dissent, sometimes validated by an appeal to the Spirit. Then, under the stress of the Napoleonic period and its aftermath, the Friends swung towards evangelicalism, which dominated their meetings until almost the end of the nineteenth century, though without enabling them to recover as a popular movement.

Wesleyanism, even in the 1740s, never became the kind of subversive perfectionist assault group which George Fox cherished in his heart but which suffered terribly after the Restoration. There was never a Wesleyan equivalent of Philadelphia, where Thomas Jefferson wrote the Declaration of Independence, nor were eighteenth-century Wesleyans hanged in the American Colonies as the Friends had been under Charles II. This was because Wesley could not bear the feeling, which did not worry Fox at all, that he was, to use a modern German word, '*asozial*'. For all his preaching forays on the margins of Anglicanism and his refusal to submit to ecclesiastical – that is, to episcopal – control, Wesley still wanted to be an insider, to be regarded as a Church of England man, and he surrendered his Oxford fellowship only when his late marriage made this inevitable. (The income from a fellowship ceased when the fellow married; this made surrender a matter of form. Wesley retained his fellowship for four years after marriage, resigning in 1755.) In the 1760s his favourite scheme for the problem of how to extend his movement was to bring the evangelical Anglican into the sphere of the contract which he had imposed on his itinerants, who were told regularly that they retained a liberty to withdraw from him, but not a liberty to criticise him, even in the annual ministerial Conference.

There was a further element of eccentricity in Wesley's theology. In *Thoughts on Christian Perfection*, published in 1759–60, he told his readers that if they believed they had died to sin they should 'undoubtedly' say so. In 1762, when

the London troubles were still going on and before George
Bell had brought matters to a head by indulging in prophecy,
Wesley warned everyone against 'stillness: ceasing in a wrong
sense from your own works. To mention one instance out of
many: "You have received", says one, "a great blessing. But
you began to talk of it and to do this and that; and so you lost
it. You should have been still."' The passage is obscure, but
Wesley appears to mean that those who do not make their radically changed spiritual condition publicly known risk the loss
of the gift. In later perfectionist revivalism it was often said
that those who did not testify would lose the gift of imparted
holiness, and Wesley may have had this in mind in 1762. What
no one ever denied, however, in the long run, was that those
who claimed the possession of holiness invariably lost it – that
is, lost the altered state of consciousness which had become the
hallmark of the experience. Accounts of personal perfection
are always set in the past, as in the case of the stories the itinerants published in the *Arminian Magazine* in the 1770s, and did
not usually cover a great length of time. There was a subjective sense of transformation, which looks like dissociation, or
a kind of quasi-trance experience, from which normality suddenly returned, often as the result of some behavioural jolt:
the individual, assuming deliverance from an old habit such as
anger, suddenly found anger had taken control, and the sense
of freedom, of dispensing love in moral liberality, vanished.

Wesley's teaching on holiness marked off his territory from
that of the established Church. There is a hearsay reference in the correspondence of the evangelical poet William
Cowper (1731–1800) which suggests that John Fletcher, in a
sermon preached in the parish church of the Yorkshire town of
Dewsbury, had outraged the local parson by identifying being
a true Christian with being perfected, and had then asserted
that he was both.[36] The vicar had refused to allow Fletcher

to preach in the Dewsbury pulpit again. Cowper, who was writing to another well-known evangelical Anglican, John Newton (1725–1807), whom he had helped to compile the distinctly unWesleyan *Olney Hymns* (1779), observed that he knew of Fletcher's pious reputation and could hardly believe what he had been told. What is significant about this story is the horror with which, as late as 1781, the evangelical Anglicans reacted to the idea of 'perfection', whether as theory or as fact.

3

Later Wesleyanism: 1770–1800

In the second half of the eighteenth century Wesleyan membership increased and was to go on increasing in the United Kingdom and United States for a long time. In the same period the movement began to lose its more eccentric characteristics and to seek, as its institutional shell hardened, a new and less evangelical satisfaction in respectability.

Membership statistics are hard to come by for the first generation of Wesleyanism; in 1748 the annual Conference, made up entirely of itinerants and ministerial sympathisers from other bodies, especially the Church of England, was informed in broad terms that the movement was now divided into nine geographical divisions, which included Wales (represented at this time by only a few places in the south of the country) and Ireland (where stations existed at Dublin, Tullamore, Tyrrell's Pass and Athlone).

In England the London region, which was always to stand at the head of the returns, stretched to Oxford, Reading and Salisbury in the west, as well as encompassing Essex, Kent and Surrey. Bristol, similarly, included Bath and Devizes, and reached down through Taunton to Cullompton in Devon; the third large district, Cornwall, took in the deeper South-West, as far as St Ives. After ten years of effort, Wesleyanism appeared thinly scattered in the South-East, apart from London, but extended more firmly from Bristol into a predominantly

western region. Further north, societies ran across England
from the Cotswolds to Newcastle upon Tyne. This area
was split into four divisions: Staffordshire, which began at
Stroud and Cirencester and extended through Shrewsbury,
Leominster, Evesham and Wednesbury; Cheshire, thin on
the ground, with Nottingham, Derbyshire, Lancashire and
Sheffield recorded as circuits; Yorkshire, which in fact meant
the Leeds area, Lincolnshire and the Fens; and finally
Newcastle upon Tyne, a district which reached as far as
Berwick-upon-Tweed. The movement's continuation into a
second decade was guaranteed by the roots put down in
London, Bristol and Newcastle upon Tyne, as well as in
Cornwall, with its distinctive mining and fishing culture which
Anglicanism had never penetrated. Elsewhere the movement
looked urban rather than rural.

Official membership figures came first in 1766, by which
time these large divisions had become thirty-nine circuits.
Outside England there were four circuits in Scotland –
Edinburgh, Dundee, Aberdeen and Glasgow; two in Wales –
Glamorganshire and Pembroke; and eight in Ireland – Dublin,
Cork, Limerick, Waterford, Athlone, Castlebar, Newry and
Londonderry. As a result Scotland had four itinerants, Wales
two, and Ireland fifteen. England had seventy-one itinerants,
or nearly two to a circuit. The figures suggest how unrealistic
was Wesley's lifelong ambition to extend the movement into
countries where Anglicanism had never matched its religious
influence to its political superiority.

The area loosely covered in England had not altered very
much in twenty years. Blocks of four itinerants worked from
London, Wiltshire, Lancashire and Newcastle upon Tyne.
Haworth, in Yorkshire, where there was also strong evangeli-
cal Anglican support, had five as a separate station. Cornwall
East and Cornwall West had six in total. The small number of

the widely scattered itinerants makes obvious how much the survival of the Connexion relied on the local lay preachers and class-leaders, at the level at which many women played prominent roles (though this did not affect the overall male character of the local groups). The word 'connexion' summed up John Wesley's central authority: the itinerants existed in connexion with him.

In the 1760s Charles Wesley constantly complained to his brother about what he held to be the low quality of the majority of itinerants. He accused John of preferring 'grace', which in this case meant the ability to obtain conversions, to 'gifts', by which Charles meant administrative and intellectual qualities, combined with strength of character. This problem did not go away, and even in the 1830s, when Wesleyanism had already established itself in a middle-class environment, especially in the new northern manufacturing districts, the proposal to train itinerants in a theological college was one (though only one) of the causes of a series of secessions from the Wesleyan main body which reached a climax during 1849–57, when a once-for-all loss of momentum occurred. By the 1760s Charles Wesley believed Wesleyanism should accept that the movement had no hope either of reforming Anglicanism, or of continuing as a pietist internal opposition, more like Moravianism than Methodism. The leaders should therefore negotiate a modus vivendi with the established Church. This meant that the small group of itinerants who had gifts as well as graces would obtain episcopal ordination; Charles thought that the remainder should, literally, go home. John Wesley had himself abandoned the plan of changing the Church of England from within, but had substituted the passionate conviction that Wesleyanism must 'spread scriptural holiness throughout the land'. Graces counted for more than gifts in this task.

Wesley knew that Wesleyanism had begun to stiffen. He reacted by saying that 'many Methodists grew rich, and thereby
lovers of the present world. Next, they married unawakened
or half-awakened wives, and conversed with their relations.'
In this fashion 'prudence' and 'conformity to the world' crept
back into the societies. There followed 'gross neglect of rela-
tive duties, especially the education of young children'. Above
all, 'this is not cured by the Preachers: either they have not
light, or they have not weight enough'.[1] Wesley complained
of the preachers that they lacked the skill and the personality
to admonish and overawe their congregations.

His wider attack on the laity contained no straight historical evidence but sounds like a familiar pietist rhetorical
reaction. Money, wives and their worldly relations (an odd
silence about husbands at this point, perhaps an indirect re-
version to the story of the Fall, though we must remember
that Wesley himself had at last married only ten years before)
as well as undisciplined children: instinctively the dissatisfied
preacher attacked his own creation and asserted that the societies themselves must take the blame for failure. Satan, worsted
in previous encounters with Calvinism and Antinomianism,[2]
had tempted the members again, this time through marriage,
procreation and financial success. If they had failed, however,
this did not imply a weakness in the holiness teaching itself
but primarily a fault in the membership, and secondarily in
the itinerants.

Wesley's analysis missed the point of what was happening. The new Wesleyans welcomed the close relationships of
the societies as centres of increased religious self-absorption,
where both men and women could feel that their personal
existence had become more exciting, more socially important. Religion became a powerful source of identity. They
found great satisfaction in belonging to what constituted an

alternative society, though this had not yet become, as it became later in some parts of the North of England, an alternative establishment. The Wesleyan meeting, whether for preaching or lovefeast, still drew on the qualities of primary religion, when the air in the meeting-room grew thick with talk of answered prayer, when sudden bursts of religious excitement emerged unpredictably out of the invisible world through the surprised congregation, and the chapel rocked with lined-out singing which fused men, women and children into a single body of supplication or celebration.[3] Far into the 1850s a minority always felt that real Wesleyanism broke the rules, believed in God-given spontaneity, a radical change of heart, and a hopeful search for a simple way back to a joyous beginning. But the joyous beginning belonged to the meeting, not to the world. The rules of the world differed from those of the meeting, and the itinerants risked the loss of both light and weight if they challenged that.

In the second Wesleyan wave many of the itinerants wanted to transform themselves into Dissenting or Anglican ministers fixed in a particular parish or local chapel. They did not think of themselves as surrendering to the world, but hoped that the world might surrender to them. Wesley on the contrary wanted the Connexion to expand on the basis of holiness teaching. Reconstruction as a Dissenting body, an action which Wesley prevented in the 1770s, would have meant a new denomination of not much more than about seventy independent local centres, some of which might well have declined quite rapidly, while others would soon have become large urban chapels, fated to explode from time to time in the kind of congregational splitting and founding of a new church which had become characteristic of the Dissenting subculture. Some of the itinerants, not always the least able, liked that idea, and a few of them left Wesley for such settled pastorates.

As already noted, distinct membership figures first appeared in 1766, in the *Minutes of the Annual Conference*, although on this occasion London, Canterbury, Oxfordshire and Devon had not sent them. England, with these circuits missing, had 19,267 members in 1766; the result of twenty-eight years of campaigning, it is hardly an outcome which suggests a massive swing to primary religion. The principal centres were clear: Cornwall as a whole 2,235; Lancashire 1,742; Bristol 1,089; Leeds 1,072. Birstal with 1,376 and Haworth with 1,536 should really be taken together. Yarm returned 1,103 and Newcastle upon Tyne 1,804. The missing figures would have pushed the total above 20,000, but not above 25,000. The number of itinerants came to seventy-one, as in the previous year. In 1767 the full English total was 25,211; the membership in Wales was 232 and in Scotland 468, which underlines again the lack of success in the Wesleyan drive to penetrate these countries.

The later rate of overall expansion can be gauged by comparing the figures for 1783, towards the end of the catastrophe of the American War of Independence. England and Wales, after a further seventeen years of dedicated work, returned 39,419 members, of which South Wales brought in 487; there were 523 members in Scotland, while Ireland now presented 6,053 Wesleyans. The number of itinerants in England and Wales had doubled to 143; there were 8 in Scotland and 35 in Ireland.

It is possible to speak of an average 250 members per itinerant, but in many areas the membership was widely scattered in small groups, and the two-year system of stationing not only left no time for the itinerants to build up a following which might secede with them, but also prevented them from using their local links to draw more people into the societies. Congregations were, however, larger than membership in the eighteenth century. Moreover, this second-level attendance must slowly have pulled the Wesleyans back towards the centre from their historical origins on the Anglican margin. The additional uncommitted hearers – the Wesleyans called them adherents – counted most in the larger centres of population, and they have to be taken into consideration when deciding how far the growth of the Wesleyan movement weakened the Anglican and Dissenting Churches.

The Visitation Returns for Wiltshire, which was in the Salisbury diocese, in 1783,[4] help in picturing the rural impact of Wesleyanism towards the end of Wesley's life. A total of 232 parishes made returns, of which 155 had no kind of school and 158 had no Dissenters, a remarkable result in itself. The Returns suggest that there were about 5,000 Anglican communicants in the area covered; the Wesleyan Conference return for 1782 gave a total of 1,264 members in the districts of Bradford-on-Avon and Sarum, which together roughly corresponded to Wiltshire. Old Dissent – that is, the Baptists, Independents and Presbyterians – was recorded in seventy-four parishes, with its principal strength lying in the cloth-making towns of Bradford-on-Avon, Devizes, Malmesbury, Trowbridge, Wilton and the weaving village of North Bradley. Dissent also mattered in Marlborough, and in St Thomas's parish in Salisbury. The Society of Friends had almost disappeared.

Methodists and Moravians were mentioned in thirty-seven parishes, about one-sixth of the total. Moravianism had entered Wiltshire thanks to John Cennick's transfer of the societies he had formed in the 1740s into Moravianism from Wesleyanism. They had built chapels at Bremhill and Brinkworth, with a single minister, but hardly existed elsewhere, because their foreign leader, Count Zinzendorf,[5] had imposed a virtual ban on aggressive evangelism. No confusion of names affected these identifications: the incumbents clearly distinguished the few Moravian centres.

The Methodists, whom the parish priests thought of as belonging to a group of sects, usually flourished where Dissent was already strong, as in Devizes, Trowbridge and Wilton. It is not easy to disentangle the Wesleyans proper from those recorded as Methodists. Some of these people belonged to the Countess of Huntingdon's Connexion; and there was an evangelical Anglican group at Christian Malford, where Rowland Hill had a congregation,[6] and in the parish of St Peter's in Marlborough. Lady Huntingdon had recruited a small number of originally Anglican moderate Calvinists, whom she had established in proprietary chapels. In Marlborough the priest of St Peter's recorded that:

> the other Presbyterians are maiden ladies. The sect is greatly reduced of late years, as by marrying wives of the Church of England, so by many of them turning Methodists, who assemble in a former Presbyterian meeting-house in this parish, by the name of Independents, and licensed as such. The sect is supported, as I am informed, by Lady Huntingdon, and an opulent tradesman of this parish, who is owner of the meeting-house. Their teacher's name is Cornelius Winter, who seems to have had a liberal education, and who complains of the decrease of his hearers.

There was another Huntingdonian group at Steeple Ashton, near Trowbridge, 'who meet at a labourer's house, not licensed; preachers, one Newborn, a weaver, and one Sly, a tailor. Their numbers less by some hundreds than of late years. They are of the Huntingdonian sect.' It was also recorded that three or four families used to go from Sutton St Benger to the Christian Malford chapel, and there was 'a very small meeting' at Urchfont. That leaves more than thirty parishes in which the Wesleyans were active.

The Visitation was an Anglican document, meant for a bishop, and it leaves the impression that not much had changed in Wiltshire in the previous fifty years. The absence of schools in parish after parish helps to explain the rigidity and misery of the society as a whole. Many incumbents knew about the poverty which surrounded them. This tempted them to identify Methodism with poverty and ignorance, because this enabled them to look down on the teachers, as they invariably called the itinerants, underlining where possible that they had not licensed themselves. It is often said that by this time John Wesley had become a revered old man, but this did not affect the standing of the itinerants in a county like Wiltshire.

According to the Conference *Minutes* probably six or seven itinerants worked in this area in 1783, which would give a ratio of one to about 200 members. There were four itinerants stationed in the Salisbury circuit in 1783, but the number seems usually to have been three: St Edmund's parish in Salisbury recorded 'two Presbyterian meeting-houses and one for Methodists', but gave no other details. One of the Wesleyan itinerants in 1782 was William Moore, and the return for Chippenham simply stated that there was 'one Methodist meeting, Moore the name of the teacher but whether licensed or not cannot say. Salter, the Presbyterian teacher, licensed ... The Methodists have many who absent themselves from all public worship.' The Anglicans seem to have resented the Methodist withdrawal from the parish church, because the bishop's questions included one asking what was done about people who avoided religious services in general.

This small group of Wesleyan itinerants in Wiltshire, most of whom had probably been licensed by the 1780s, would have been invisible among the more than 200 Anglican ministers, and those who made the returns wanted to leave that impression of unimportance. Thus at Ebbesbourne Wake, in South Wiltshire, for example, we learn that the Methodists had built a chapel 'about two years since ... the names of the teachers are unknown to me ... the number of the attendants increases'.

The incumbent at Broughton Gifford near Melksham reported that some people 'spend much of their time, to the great detriment and poverty of their families, in going after ignorant itinerant preachers'. The same attitude distinguishes the comment made by the parson at Potterne: 'some Methodists assemble on Sundays for whom a low fellow preaches, but not numerous'. All these remarks were meant to give the same basic impression – that the Wesleyans were not really dangerous, even if difficult to put down. One of the most tolerant incumbents was the parish priest at Tollard Royal, near Shaftesbury, who related that 'there is a small house where a few meet to worship. They have no appointed teacher but sometimes one person sometimes another comes once a week . . . They call themselves Methodists, appear to me to be a peaceable, well-disposed people, but few in number.' Significantly, none of the Anglican returns suggests that the Methodists, whether Calvinist or Wesleyan, remained part of the Church of England.

As these returns also imply, what the incumbents were most aware of was the local preachers, a few of whom were named in the documents and whose lack of qualifications the Anglicans emphasised. The fact that these men – no mention occurs of women – preached and organised remained in the 1780s a sign of social insubordination, of personal independence, which alarmed the parsons. They feared that the bishop might interpret this lay activity as evidence of their own failure to prevent an increase in Dissent over a period when the older forms of Nonconformity seemed to the Anglicans to have declined. They wanted to minimise this setback, but they dared not conceal it altogether. Some of them felt angry not only with the wealthier lay Methodists as social traitors, men who had betrayed their own side, but also with their fellow

Anglican parsons, who had not managed to cope with what should have proved a brief episode.

This explains why the Reverend James Mayo, who had been an undergraduate at Queen's College, Oxford, in 1734, and so belonged to the same generation as John Wesley, and who had served at Avebury since 1745, was anxious to tell his bishop:

About the year 1740 Whitefield and the Wesleys broke forth from the University and – compassing heaven and earth to gain proselytes maintained . . . that the Church of England, or rather the clergy of the Church of England, had totally departed from the pure doctrines of the Gospel, and particularly those which were contained in her Homilies – which, as they asserted, were wholly laid aside and absolutely sunk in oblivion.

He had, he said, as his father's curate, read the Homilies, 'an essential blow being thereby given to the growth and establishment of Methodism in that parish'. If only everybody else had done the same, he implied, no problem would have arisen. This sounded fine but in fact Methodists of a kind did exist in Avebury; they were more likely Independents, for whom one Davis came over from Marlborough; while the Huntingdonian teacher, Cornelius Winter, used a room there from time to time.

The overall picture painted by the Wiltshire Visitation suggests some loss of Anglican confidence, but not an Anglicanism compelled by the emergence of Whitefield and the Wesleys to react to the social order differently. There were not enough Wesleyans in either the country towns or in the villages to affect the relationship between the better and worse-off sections of society. Most evangelical Anglicans retained faith in the Church of England, both the general system of establishment and the local parochial machinery. New ways of working the parish system would develop over the next fifty years or so, but the social situation would change faster and the parish would never catch up. The new device which enabled evangelical Anglicanism to transform itself into one of the three major divisions of the Church of England did not come from Wesleyanism. The key to Anglican development was the single-issue society, run on a national basis with a London Committee linked to local affiliates, a plan which came naturally to the network of evangelical businessmen, and which grew out of the choice in the 1780s of the slave trade and slavery as the proper targets for the movement.

From the perspective of some of the more deprived parts of Wiltshire in the 1780s the choice of slavery may have looked ironic, as did its complement, the Church Missionary Society of 1799, which busied itself with worlds far distant from Wiltshire. Evangelical Anglicanism responded not so much to new religious possibilities in Africa, India and the West Indies as to a new phase in English nationalism, which rebounded from the loss of the American War of Independence and the threats of further spoliation in the French Revolutionary Wars with a determination, if not to dictate the terms of the peace, at least to take advantage of the missionary chances offered by military and political victory. Wesleyanism would follow suit, starting its own official Missionary Society in 1818, and going on to display unhesitating support for the Victorian empire.

By the 1790s it was the evangelicals, rather than the second wave of Wesleyans, who showed signs of trying to change society outside their own boundaries, of coping with the problems which the Wiltshire Visitation, for example, had exposed, however indirectly. Hannah More (1745–1833), an evangelical Anglican intellectual and writer, prompted by William Wilberforce (1759–1833), the most prominent and highly politicised member of the group, tried to tackle the problems of rural poverty and ignorance in north Somerset, where there was a similar absence of village schools to that recorded in Wiltshire, and where industrial development – in mining, for example – was creating a new race of the industrial poor. The setting up of schools had political roots in anxiety that peasant ignorance would lead to violence, but the planting of a school in every parish, as part of the normal equipment of an up-to-date incumbent, spread rapidly through the Church of England.

Wesleyanism, on the other hand, was still torn between primary religious activities and the pursuit of preferably urban stability in large respectable chapels. The confusion showed itself in Bristol, for example, in 1788, when the vicar of the central Temple church in Bristol was helped by six Wesleyan preachers to exorcise George Lukins, a tailor from Yatton.[7] Horace Walpole (1717–97), a sophisticated mocker of the religion of his contemporaries, but also, improbably, Hannah More's regular correspondent, was delighted, and wrote to her: 'What an abominable mummery has been acting there by the Methodists with their exorcism.'[8] Hannah More replied deploring the foolishness of the times: 'The divining-rod is still considered as oracular in many places. Devils are cast out by seven ministers: and to complete the disgraceful catalogue, slavery is vindicated in print, and defended in the House of Peers. Poor human reason, when wilt thou come to years of discretion?'[9] Walpole was amused and replied approving of her attitude: 'I delight too in the temperature of your piety, and that you would not see the enthusiastic exorcist.' He continued:

I much doubt whether any chaplain of the regiments we have sent to India had once whispered to a native of Bengal, that there are milder forms of government than those of his country – no; security of property is not a wholesome doctrine to be inculcated in a land where the soil produces diamonds and gold – In short, if your Bristol exorcist believes he can cast out devils, why does he not go to Leadenhall Street [the headquarters of the East India Company]? There is a company whose name is legion.[10]

These letters underline the gap between the Wesleyans and the more sophisticated evangelical Anglicans; John Wesley was still alive, though eighty-five by this time and not personally involved. Such events do not, however, altogether entitle one to go as far as Michael Macdonald, an authority on the historical study of anxiety and healing in the eighteenth century, who has claimed that 'orthodox hostility to religious therapy deepened during the eighteenth century, when John and Charles Wesley enhanced the popular following of the Methodists by curing mad people and the putative victims of diabolical possession and witchcraft'.[11] Charles Wesley had dissociated himself from such practices long before the 1780s. John's religious therapy hovered on the borderline between sense and nonsense: he did sometimes diagnose a struggle between the power of demons and the power of prayer under the general supervision of God. The strength of the primary religious impulse involved here can be gauged from the fact that a few months before she died in 1997, Mother Teresa, one of the most prominent figures in twentieth-century Roman Catholicism, was exorcised in Calcutta, because her carers thought she was being attacked by the devil.

A further source of the gap between the evangelical clergy and the Wesleyans may be found in the controversy about whether a member of the societies should attend the parish church if this meant hearing the preaching of an unevangelical (in the Wesleyan sense) or anti-Wesleyan minister. Wesley hesitated to direct his followers not to listen to such parsons, because this would have cut them off from attendance at Anglican holy communion on indefensible grounds.

The validity of the sacramental service did not theologically depend on the character of the person who administered the ordinance, but directly on an act of God. Withdrawal would also increase doubts as to whether the Wesleyans could still call themselves Anglicans. In a sermon published in 1750, whose text was: 'Beware of false prophets' (Matthew 7: 1), Wesley concluded with scathing irony: 'Even by those who are under a curse themselves God can and doth give us his blessing. For the bread which they break we have experimentally [that is, as a matter of experience] known to be the communion of the body of Christ; and the cup which God blessed, even by their unhallowed lips, was to us the communion of the blood of Christ.'[12] Wesley knew that many Wesleyans rejected his argument, and he felt obliged to add that those in doubt must pray and 'then act according to the best light you have', for 'if by experience you find that the hearing of them hurts your soul, then hear them not; then quietly refrain, and hear those who profit you'. In his edition of Wesley's sermons (from which the extracts above are taken) A. C. Outler commented that what he called Wesley's toleration was rooted in his ecclesiology, but if this was so it was not, historically speaking, Anglican ecclesiology, and what Wesley said permitted a conscientious Wesleyan to abstain from Anglican communion, on the ground that the local parson either preached an unfaithful gospel or lived a scandalous life. Wesley's toleration, if that is what it was, did not lead to tolerance among his followers: refusal of Anglican communion strengthened the demand that the itinerants should administer the sacrament themselves, which happened increasingly in the 1770s and 1780s. Wesley concluded his advice with a 'few plain words' aimed at 'false prophets'. He attacked them from the emotional heart of the Wesleyan movement:

Can you possibly believe that God hath sent you? That ye are his messengers? Nay, if the Lord had sent you, the work of the Lord would prosper in your hands. As the Lord liveth, if ye were messengers of God he would confirm the work of his messengers. But the work of the Lord doth not prosper in your hands: you bring no sinners to repentance. The Lord doth not confirm your word, for you save no souls from death.

Here, as so often, the ability to convert people became the test that counted. When Wesley used language which implied reforming the Church of England, he meant that he wanted to change the preaching of many of the parish clergy; he had no structural alterations in mind. The cult of conversion stretched as far as sometimes allowing women to preach, and this also widened the gap between the two bodies.

Anglican authority remained unmoved. Professor Frank Baker's *John Wesley and the Church of England* (1970) provided a detailed discussion of the relationship between the Establishment and Wesleyanism, but, as its title implies, concentrated on Wesley rather than the Wesleyans, and so distorted the problem. The bishops themselves disliked a system in which laymen preached and women sometimes prophesied. They sincerely believed in the need for an educated ministry, or or at least a ministry which had gone through Oxford or Cambridge, for what that was worth in the eighteenth century. A version of the Roman Catholic seminary for training priests had to wait until the nineteenth century, and in practice the eighteenth-century clergyman could be as unprepared for service as an eighteenth-century Army officer. There was little training for the pastoral office in the Hanoverian university, though the ordinands usually became aware of the gap between a secular and a set-apart existence, and sometimes tried, as the Oxford Methodists had, to work out a pattern of clerical behaviour for themselves. What they were taught stressed the value of classical texts, of written authority at the expense of observation, and did not encourage attention to eighteenth-century philosophy.

To say that the eighteenth-century bishops had no policy towards the upsurge of Wesleyanism, a view that goes back at least as far as John Henry Newman, is incorrect: they would have limited its growth, even stopped it altogether, if they could, but they lacked the power. They clearly saw no point in opening official negotiations with Wesley: they abhorred his enthusiasm for primary religion, distrusted the nature of his secondary theology, and had no confidence in his character. It is significant that no group which did negotiate with Wesley united with him: the Moravians, the evangelical Anglicans, the Countess of Huntingdon's Connexion, all kept their distance and their liberty of action. The episcopate must have known about this manoeuvring and have drawn their own conclusions.

John Wesley's ostentatious loyalty to the Hanoverian dynasty in 1745, his aggressive support for English rule in Ireland, and his eagerness to back the Crown against the American colonists, no doubt help to explain the respectability which he enjoyed as an old man. His Toryism was self-evident, and for a while Toryism was popular. He had not set out with consciously political intentions in the 1740s, but the temptation to give his views on political crises grew stronger with age. His ill-judged publications in the period which followed the passing of the Roman Catholic Relief Act in the summer of 1778, and his reponse to the events which culminated in the anti-Catholic Gordon Riots of 1780, showed that he rebelled against the official (and moderate Anglican) policy of bringing English Roman Catholics into the civil community and closer to a consensus of the political elites. This cannot have benefited his reputation with the episcopate.

Wesley was seventy-seven in 1780, and he was repeating lifelong anti-Catholic opinions. His language at that time carried less emotional impact than his frequent denunciations of both Moravians, towards whom he was unsparing, and Calvinists, who gave as good as they got in return. He certainly did not think of his words as having physical consequences, though he supported the retention of anti-Catholic legislation. But he had never acted as a mediator between the changing elite culture of eighteenth-century England on the one hand, and those, not all socially inferior, who did not want social or intellectual change, and who in religious terms preferred the traditional possibilities of an interventionist deity. Intellectually, though very self-assured, Wesley had no idea of bridging the gap between his ideas and words and those of the bishops, moderate Calvinists, liberal Anglicans and sceptics who disagreed with him. From the Anglican episcopal point of view he and his followers remained a potentially disruptive political force well into the 1780s, and the American War of Independence increased the mistrust.

Once again, it is important to distinguish between Wesley and the Wesleyans. Wesley's political opinions, which were firmly conservative, did not carry excessive weight in the Wesleyan societies, as a study of the Wesleyan society in Bristol in 1784, for example, shows.[13] Bristol offers an excellent example of eighteenth-century urban Wesleyanism, distinct from other centres such as Leeds or Newcastle upon Tyne. The society had 790 members. Women predominated: about 524, which amounted to two-thirds. The largest groups were servants (55), shoemakers (47), washerwomen (26) and sempstresses (24). There were 29 gentlemen and gentlewomen (21 of them women), and 25 women described variously as poor, old or almswomen. Among the local leaders were John Castleman, a surgeon, and Henry Durbin, a chemist. There were also the printers Marshall Pine and William Bulgin, who started a printing firm with Roland Rosser in the 1780s, and who all printed for Wesley. Joseph Edwards was probably the youngest member of the family who had a prosperous clay tobacco-pipe business which operated from 70 Temple Street from 1775 to 1823. Many other members earned a living in the characteristic local trades – glass, pottery, shipping and so forth.

The Bristol Poll Book of 1784 makes possible certain observations on the political nature of the Bristol Wesleyans.[14] In the election of 1784 the Bristol result was: Matthew Brickdale (Tory) 3,458; Henry Cruger (Whig) 3,052; George Daubeny (Tory) 2,982; Sam Peach (Whig) 373. Brickdale retained his seat; Daubeny lost his seat to Cruger. A vote for Brickdale and Daubeny might be interpreted as a vote for the monarchy and for British and Bristolian interests in North America. Not long before, in January 1782, Wesley had passionately defended George III, pointing out that the Bible plainly commanded: 'Thou shalt not speak evil of the ruler of thy people' (Exodus 22: 28). He extended the application of the text to the king's ministers and generals, who were being criticised for every defeat in America. When ministers were censured without reason, and odium cast on the king by that means, it was, he said, the duty of a Christian minister to preach politics.[15] Wesley would have liked his followers to vote Tory, but it is evident that they followed their own inclinations. A number of Wesleyan voters in 1784 can be identified with reasonable certainty. The list included two grocers, two tailors, two cordwainers, two labourers, a schoolmaster and an 'accomptant'. The small sample shows a broad correspondence to the overall result. There is no evidence here for a specific Wesleyan influence on this particular poll. Thirty-eight Wesleyans seem to have voted, sixteen for Brickdale, eleven for Daubeny, the

Tory candidates; eleven voted for Cruger, who took second place. The votes for Brickdale and Daubeny, most of them plumpers, were in line with Wesley's support for the king and Lord North in the American War of Independence, but the votes for Cruger showed that his example was limited.

Most of the Anglican bishops wanted to be a part of a politer, more rational society, and they valued their closeness to the throne and their role, which had begun to decline, in the House of Lords. They believed as strongly as Wesley did in the value of social subordination, of a monarchical country governed by elites, but they did not accept Wesley's opinion that his societies reinforced this traditional order. They thought that Wesley as an ordinary Anglican minister should subordinate himself to them, and that in practice he was building a Nonconformist religious movement which challenged the existence of the established Church. The most prominent Wesleyan figures were known to assert that they had recovered the true faith of Anglican Protestantism, and to add that many of the beneficed clergy knew nothing of it. So Wesleyanism was left in, rather than driven into, a sort of social wilderness between Old Dissent and the Church of England.

Wesleyans began to benefit from this social alienation when what had been small market towns, like Bradford in Yorkshire, started to expand as industrial centres.[16] Wesleyanism coped well with the early phases of this economic and social change because its societies were not imposing a radical religious break with the primary religion of the past, but constructing a cultural shelter which appealed to many people who felt as though they were looking for asylum in their own country, and who were searching not only for work but also for ways to reconcile themselves to a new environment. Wesleyanism was one way in which the sufferers themselves improvised order on the spot out of potential chaos. But the Anglican hierarchy, close to the political state and to *la vie mondaine* but remote from the places in the community where change caused the most pain, was chiefly sensitive to the bizarre side of the new organisation.

Some of the surviving papers of George Lavington (1684–1762), the mid eighteenth-century bishop of Exeter, throw light on how the episcopate groped for an understanding of Wesleyanism.[17] He based his *Enthusiasm of Methodists and Papists Compared* (1749–51)[18] on the information he gathered from a circle of clerical and lay correspondents, not all of them in his diocese. Parts of what Lavington received might fairly be called 'scurrilous', the epithet of some Wesleyan commentators, but this is not true of the whole. Strictly speaking, this material relates to the first wave of Wesleyanism, but the correspondence is so typical of the difficulties the Church of England faced throughout the century that it fits in naturally at this point. Lavington had been stung by the distribution in his diocese of an anonymous version of a Visitation charge which he had given to his clergy. In the forged version he was said to have told them to stop preaching mere morality and to preach instead Christ crucified in the Methodist style.

Thoroughly outraged, he had sought opinions from both sides of the ecclesiastical divide. Some of those who replied took the Wesleyan side. For example, one of his respondents was the Reverend T. Vivian (1720–93), of Redruth. Vivian was a young man sympathetic to John Wesley at this stage of the movement, though thirty years later Wesley described him as one who had fallen 'into the pit of the decrees, and knows me no more' (see the *Arminian Magazine* 1778), in other words, a Calvinist. Vivian distinguished between the committed Wesleyans and their hangers-on; he complained that the faults of behaviour of the latter were attributed to the societies as a whole. He had already, I suspect, written to Lavington a favourable description of the Wesleyans in which he had remarked that they 'profess that they can live without committing sin', perfectionist language which did not appeal to Lavington. Vivian added that their distinguishing principle 'and the only one wherein they say that they differ from the Church, is what they call Sensible Justification', which they described as 'such a sense of his love towards them as is always accompanied with great peace and sometimes with joy'. The Wesleyans, he noted, were also known as constant reprovers of other people's conduct. These statements come from a document which has lost its signature, but whose handwriting seems identical with Vivian's. The last point reminds one of the Society of Friends, but also of Wesley, who regarded reproof as a duty. What reproof could mean in pietist circles is exemplified by an anonymous letter to Lavington which attacked him for allowing his wife and daughters to go to the playhouse, conduct held to be contrary to the gospel.

Episcopal behaviour was a difficult issue at the time, and it is helpful to fast-forward and compare this criticism with Samuel Johnson's views on episcopal manners in 1781. Boswell reported that Johnson was offended because Jonathan Shipley, the bishop of St Asaph, had been elected a member of the famous conversation Club (later the Literary Society), which met at the Turk's Head in Gerrard Street in London. There was nothing unusual about the meeting-place, but Johnson said: ' "A bishop has nothing to do at a tippling house . . . There is nothing immoral in it . . . There are gradations. There is morality, decency, propriety . . . A bishop should not go to a house where he may meet a man leading out a whore." ' He also, according to Boswell, found fault with Beilby Porteus, then bishop of Chester but to become bishop of London in 1787, for going to routs and staying too long at them. ' "He may go to them," said he, "and receive attentive respect while

it is paid him. But when that ceases, he is then to retire."
Mrs Thrale said that "the bishop of Chester is never minded
[heeded] at a rout".' Whereupon Boswell himself added that
'when a bishop is in a state where he is nobody, it is improper'.
Johnson agreed.[19] What was at stake was not the bishop's
moral character, but the protection of his decorum, or, as the
Conversation Club put it, the preservation of decency and
propriety. This might apply as much to episcopal daughters
as to the bishops themselves.

Vivian's pro-Wesleyan note was also struck in a correspondence which Lavington had with J. Stonhouse of
Northampton, a town in which Philip Doddridge (1702–51)
had served as an Independent minister from 1730, and where he
had organised a famous Dissenting academy; a Wesleyan society did not form there until 1767 and still had only fifty-five
members in 1793. Stonhouse insisted, in a letter written in
October 1748, that an astonishing reformation would take
place in the land, 'if the Gospel were earnestly and properly preached'. He hinted that he knew who had circulated
the anonymous version of Lavington's Visitation charge, but
did not want to reveal who was responsible. In an earlier
letter Stonhouse wrote that he had not intended to 'insinuate
any Pretensions [on the part of the Wesleyans] to immediate
Revelation, or extraordinary Inspiration' but, as he evidently
could not resist adding – and that was symptomatic as well –
'there is a sense in which Christ promises to come and manifest
himself to everyone that loves him and keeps his Word John
xiv 21, which I presume signify his giving by the influence of
his Spirit a lively apprehension of his Presence and Grace'.
No doubt Lavington objected to this description of religious
experience, as well as to the sweeping dismissal of Anglican
preaching in general.

The strength of the episcopal reaction to such defences of
Wesleyanism can be seen in an exchange of letters between

Lavington and John Conybeare, who was bishop of Bristol from 1750 until his death in 1755. Lady Huntingdon was seeking ordination for one of her protégés, Richard Eliot. Conybeare, assuring Lavington that he would not ordain Eliot, laid it down that 'of all men an Enthusiast is the most unfit to officiate in the church', and added that in Bristol it was hoped that once a new church building had been completed in Kingswood, 'this madness [Wesleyanism] will be in great measure extinguished' (5 September 1752). Lavington answered that enthusiasm would do less mischief out of the Church than in it (21 December 1752). Wesleyanism survived in Kingswood.

Lavington's intention as a polemicist was to assert that there was a suspicious similarity between new Wesleyanism and old Romanism. At the level of theological and liturgical detail he could not make his claims good, because the two bodies simply did not resemble one another. Lavington, however, was not being malicious, or writing out of an inability to appreciate 'gospel religion' when he encountered it. A similarity did exist between Wesleyanism and English Catholicism, though the bishop failed to put his finger on it. The likeness lay in the relationship both movements had to primary religious impulses. Both inhabited a narrative full of heightened feeling and providential intervention, though by the 1770s Wesleyanism had started to leave its radical beginnings behind, whereas English Catholicism was acquiring more confidence in its handling of primary religious activities such as the invocation of the saints in its dealings with mainstream society. And one can make an extended parallel between Catholic visions of the Virgin Mary and the Wesleyan attachment to visions of the crucified Jesus, and even of the Father. In both cases the images or pictures supplied a new and apparently decisive context for the text itself. There was therefore more to the Anglican episcopal reaction to the expansion of Wesleyanism in the second half of the eighteenth century than can be summed up in the traditional contrast between 'enthusiasm' and 'moral preaching', a contrast in which 'preaching morality' is always made to sound inferior to 'preaching the gospel'.

The question Lavington raised we might now put in different words, and ask what exactly was the social and moral value, let alone the the religious significance, of satisfying the need for images, for specific healing, for material reward, for emotional release. From the bishops' point of view, 'enthusiasm' meant making claims that could not be substantiated: these included not only Wesleyan claims about 'knowing that one had been forgiven' and about the possibility of perfect holiness, but also the assertions, made by the Calvinist groups in general, about predestination and election. The bishops regarded both as pride and self-delusion, and they did not think that ordinary men and women should be encouraged to talk about themselves in this fashion. This criticism constituted the fundamental ground for proclaiming the value of 'moral preaching', of teaching men and women their obligations to social order and subordination, and to the earnest pursuit of the good as far as in them lay. There was no chance, in eighteenth-century terms, of reconciling this humane Anglican attitude with the radical suspicion of all human effort which coloured the favourable use of the word 'enthusiasm'.

Let us now look more closely at the Wesleyan itinerants, who so signally failed to impress either the parsons or the bishops. By the 1770s the itinerants saw themselves as religious professionals, part of an administrative as well as a preaching class, set apart above all to preach, and in no religious sense inferior to the regular clergy. Wesley felt obliged to come to terms with these feelings. In 1784, with the American War of Independence lost, and the colonial Church of England in complete disarray, he reinvented his own theology of the professional ministry in order to justify himself in ordaining, in what he declared to be a fully valid manner, men who were to be called 'Wesleyan Methodist pastors or ministers'. The bishops were bound to reject, as outside the Anglican tradition (to which he still insisted he was loyal) his assertion that Church of England presbyters like himself were as entitled to ordain as bishops. Nevertheless, in conjunction with Thomas Coke (1747–1814) and James Creighton (1739–1819), both of whom had Anglican orders and both of whom had clashed with episcopal authority in the past, he ordained two itinerants for the United States. He went further, ordaining Coke as what he called a 'superintendent', which Coke took to mean bishop; and it is from Coke's ordination of Francis Asbury (1745–1816), who never doubted his right to style himself a bishop, that the American Methodist Episcopal Church stemmed. Asbury turned out to be the successful leader of a third wave of Wesleyanism for whom no equivalent could be found in England.

In 1785 Wesley ordained men for Scotland whom he regarded as 'unordained' in England, and in 1788 he finally overcame his hesitation and ordained Alexander Mather (1733–1800) for England itself. Mather thought of himself as the English equivalent of Asbury, but his fellow itinerants disliked Wesley's personalised centralism and refused to have a 'superintendent' in the driving-seat, preferring the honorary control of an annually appointed president. From 1795 onwards the itinerants, with wide support from the laity, assumed they were entitled to administer the Last Supper, and that the annual Conference of itinerants could appoint fresh Wesleyan ministers, and so keep the movement growing. Until the 1830s Wesleyanism remained unclear as to how exactly the Conference appointed these new men, but most of the new pastors felt they had been at least implicitly ordained. Then, when reactionary Anglo-Catholics renewed the eighteenth-century episcopal rejection of the pastoral claims of the Wesleyan itinerants, the majority of the societies sensibly supported the view that Wesleyan ordination was as valid as any other.

Wesley's ordinations had had a political intention, or overtone, because he wanted to safeguard the full-time itinerant control of the societies and so preserve what he thought should be a nondemocratic ecclesiastical body. For many years the Wesleyan Conference reflected the kind of Hanoverian sociopolitical conservatism which swore by the changeless superiority of the country's inherently aristocratic constitution, that is, the division of power arrived at between the king and the landowning elites in 1688. Wesleyanism became independent, but it did not become Dissenting; it did not become Anglican, but neither did it become politically radical. This intention lay behind the Deed of Declaration, which Wesley had drawn up in 1784, and which defined the final Wesleyan authority after his death as 100 members of the itinerancy – about half the total – whom he himself nominated with power to maintain that number. But the remainder of the itinerants allowed only a primacy of honour to the Legal Hundred, as they came to be called, and insisted on their own right to attend the Conference, in which majority voting ruled.

Wesley distinguished firmly between Dissent and his own centralised system of government over a national network of circuits whose buildings belonged to the whole Wesleyan body, not to the local trustees. Dissent was pictured as a free association between local churches which basically governed themselves and certainly owned their own buildings. Wesley did not want a Presbyterian, let alone an Independent, church order. As the itinerants accustomed themselves to living without him, they also turned away from Dissent; they attributed to themselves the kind of power which a parish priest nominally had over his parishioners, and their determination to retain this authority into the middle of the nineteenth century had disastrous results. What matters most is that whenever they had to choose, either individually or as a body, between Nonconformity and the Church of England, they preferred the Church of England. As far as possible the majority of Wesleyans refused to see themselves as inhabitants of what was still in the 1790s the socially marginal estate of Dissent.

This became even clearer after 1797, when the first of several secessions from Wesleyanism took place. Two of the itinerants, Alexander Kilham (1762–98), who had been expelled from the Connexion in 1796 because of his hostility to the pro-Anglican policy, and William Thom (1751–1811), organised a withdrawal of about one-twentieth of the membership – some 5,000 people – and set up the Methodist New Connexion, which had sixty societies scattered through the smaller manufacturing towns of the Midlands and the North. Despite the inclusion of laymen in its annual Conference, and open opposition to the Church of England, the New Connexion failed to shake either the form or change the attitudes of Wesleyanism proper. The chief reason for this was that the New Connexion did not represent a fresh infusion of primary religious energy into the Methodist subculture: the majority of the Wesleyans were content to occupy a middle-ground between Dissent and the Church of England.

This interpretation may seem to exaggerate the importance of not being a Dissenter, but it is easy to underestimate the complexity of eighteenth-century reactions. When the twenty-eight-year-old Duncan Wright (1736–91), a Scottish soldier who became a Wesleyan itinerant in 1764, was still in the Army and serving in a disturbed Ireland in the earlier 1760s, he was already preaching to a gathered congregation in his regiment. His major, he later recalled, thought it was a disgrace to have a sergeant a preacher and so intrigued (successfully in the end) for his discharge. Some of the other officers were friendly, 'for they had no trouble with the Methodist soldiers, but enough with the others. Yet they told me what they feared our enthusiasm would turn to; and mentioned Cromwell, who could preach and pray one part of the day, and kill and plunder the other.'[20] In his memoirs Wright made no more of the reference to Cromwell – hardly a name to mention casually in Ireland – and instead attacked the 'sinecure' chaplains attached to the Hanoverian Army. For his officers Methodism meant Dissent, and Dissent meant potential disaffection and violence. Whatever one says about British nationalism in the eighteenth century, England itself was not yet a single nation with an undivided, organic, undivisive history. Dissent remained unreconciled to the political decisions taken in 1688, and many of the Army officers translated this hostility into possible disloyalty.

What was this small professional group of itinerants – never more than about 200 even at the end of the century – like in general? The most direct evidence comes in *The Lives of the Early Methodist Preachers*, edited and published by Thomas Jackson in the 1840s, largely from the edited autobiographical material which John Wesley had included in the *Arminian Magazine* from 1778.[21] Only one of the itinerants who contributed, Matthias Joyce, born in 1754, belonged to the second wave proper. These men were bound together by common experience, above all by the fact that local, sporadic crowd violence aimed at preventing them from preaching occurred well into the 1760s, and ceased only as Wesley agreed that they might license themselves as Dissenting preachers, so bringing themselves more clearly under the protection of the law, without committing them in practice to a social position (the Wiltshire Visitation shows how little Dissenting status impressed Anglican observers). This sense of living together in a dangerous world was increased by the satirical attacks which had still not completely stopped in the 1770s. A. M. Lyles suggested that the peaks of satire came in 1739, 1760, 1772 and 1778, when five of the most vitriolic attacks on Wesleyan Methodism appeared.[22] One has the impression of men who, like the Friends of the previous century, prized above everything else mental and spiritual obstinacy and physical endurance.

This total group of thirty-seven men whose essays appeared in the *Magazine* included men whose origin was Scottish Presbyterian (Mather, Taylor, Wright), one Anabaptist (Payne), and one Irish Roman Catholic (Joyce), but the overwhelming majority had an Anglican background. Several were the sons of small farmers; otherwise, they were mostly small tradesmen or employees, with backgrounds in building, baking, mining (Rodda from Cornwall) and cutlery (Staniforth from Sheffield). There was an influential group of soldiers, some of whom had known each other in the Army (Cownley, Haime, Mitchell, Staniforth) and who had seen service in Europe as well as in Ireland and Scotland. There were a few who stood out for other reasons as well, such as John Pawson (1737–1806), who, it is tempting to say, had a very good opinion of himself, or Joseph Cownley (1721–92), who had money (he had married it in Cork).

Most of these men wanted to make some progress in the world and had started with little scope to do so. Wesleyanism offered them an opportunity. As a whole, they were quite unlike the tiny group of Anglican clergymen who worked with John Wesley, who regarded the itinerants as for the most part their social and educational inferiors, and who found a vocal leader in Charles Wesley. The *Lives* makes it clear that a gap in education did exist between this Anglican minority and all but a very few of the itinerants, because the Anglicans had been at a university.[23] This advantage may have been of doubtful worth in the eighteenth century, but in their case it certainly bestowed a kind of social grooming, and some accquaintance with the classics, whereas the itinerants had to content themselves with what teaching was available to them locally and supplement it with self-education. They relied heavily on the material supplied by John Wesley's Book Room, which included the controversial writings published during the interminable conflicts with the Calvinists and the Moravians. The fundamental gap between the clergy and the itinerants was social, though. The Wesleyan soldiers, for example, had not been officers, and farmers' sons were not the social equal of the tithe-receiving parsons.

The itinerants were liable to change stations every year, though Wesley, who had the last word, did not always insist. This steady rotation through wide tracts of the country from preaching-place to preaching-place, putting up in the houses of the 'friends' (a word the Wesleyans borrowed from the Quakers), also limited their social skills. They became locked into a biblical culture of their own, isolated men who depended on one another. Not untypical of their mind-set was the comment of Thomas Hanson (1733–1804), the son of a clothier from Wakefield, on the education he had received between the ages of nineteen and twenty-three. It had included some Latin and Greek. 'As soon as I left this place I laid these studies aside, and resumed them no more to this day [1780]. I have since had other work, and could not see any absolute need of these in the particular service to which I was providentially called.'[24] Alexander Mather openly criticised the amount of time his fellow itinerants gave to improving their education:

Not that I think that our brethren who have made this progress have not been useful [a key word in the Wesleyan vocabulary, here with the sense 'useful at awakening, converting and building up souls'] . . . but I think they are not more useful than they were when they were strangers to these things. And I doubt whether they are so useful as they might have been had they employed the same time, thought and diligence in the several branches of the work for which they willingly gave up all.[25]

Few Anglican ministers would even have understood this argument, but the Connexional prestige of the preachers came from 'seeing the results of their preaching', and sustaining visible links with the primary religious tradition. The rather unsatisfactory Matthias Joyce, for example, a printer born in Dublin in 1754 and brought up a Roman Catholic, whom Wesley accepted into the itinerancy in 1783, went to Cashel in that year and was distressed at 'not having so many seals to my ministry as I expected'.[26] George Shadford, who was born in Kirton in Lincolnshire in 1738, and converted in 1762, said that many times when he had been praying for his mother, 'she hath been like a person convulsed: at other times like a woman in labour, travailling through the pangs of the new birth'.[27] In some of their individual accounts the itinerants recorded the exact number of additional members brought in during their year in a circuit. The figures could be large and change dramatically. James Rogers, for example, who was born at Marsk in the North Riding of Yorkshire in 1749 and itinerated from 1772, spent the years 1775 to 1777 in Edinburgh. He reported that 'very little fruit appeared at the end of two years. We found 260 members in the Edinburgh circuit; we joined upwards of two hundred more, and yet, in the end, left only 245, that is, fifteen less than we found. So fluctuating was that people. Yet we have a few steady, faithful, hospitable friends in Scotland.'[28]

Nevertheless, by the close of the Napoleonic Wars itinerants such as William Bramwell (1759–1818),[29] who entered all his circuits determined to 'have a revival', and who shared the casual attitude of primary religion to conventional order, found themselves in conflict with their colleagues' enthusiasm for institutions. The Conference recorded of George Storey, a West Riding printer born in 1738 who itinerated from 1763 and took over the management of the Printing Office and the *Magazine* after Wesley's death, that 'he believed and loved our doctrines, which he considered as being those of the Scriptures; and perfectly approved of our discipline, and took all opportunities of enforcing it'.[30] What began as the religious aspect of the formation of an alternative society became the construction of Wesleyanism as a new religious denomination. By the close of the eighteenth century a new, closely related subculture had developed, which would last for about 200 years.

These autobiographical accounts showed a common pattern, which owed a little to seventeenth-century models of spiritual autobiography but related closely to the circumstances in which the professional group had formed. The itinerants exhibited their conformity, for example, to the theory of religious growth which they had been advocating, and therefore described their own youthful wickedness, conviction of sin, and experience of forgiveness and sometimes of sanctification. Wesley wanted to give his readers examples of the second blessing. For example, Alexander Mather wrote in 1780 that in Rotherham in 1757 he had enjoyed, as the result of 'an instantaneous deliverance from all those wrong tempers and affections which I had long and sensibly groaned under', an 'uninterrupted communion with God whether sleeping or waking'.[31] He meant, among other things, that he had no erotic dreams. Other contributors revealed how much they shared the primary religious impulses of their members, pointing out how they, too, had enjoyed providential intervention, visions of Jesus and prophetic dreams. The autobiographies also confirm that the itinerants believed that most Anglican ministers did not understand 'vital religion'. By the 1770s, however, the preachers' priority was to create and strengthen a network of societies across the United Kingdom. Within that network they fostered an anti-intellectual and democratic climate, insisting that the preachers have basic equality one with another.

A good example of the rank and file of the preachers was Samson Staniforth. Born in Sheffield in 1720, Staniforth served as a soldier for more than fifteen years, then after his discharge in 1756/7 returned successfully to baking, the trade to which he had been apprenticed as a teenager (although his father was a cutler). His vivid account of the Fontenoy campaign was less indulgent of authority than John Haime's. In Staniforth's opinion the Army was led by a self-indulgent officer class who could not organise the feeding of their men properly, expecting them to steal and pillage in order to stay alive, which was Army practice then and long after. At the battle of Fontenoy he thought that the troops had been treated as cannon fodder. If a soldier in this unsupportive environment found himself in an acute state of depression and anxiety about himself (as Staniforth did) the Army chaplaincy service gave him no help, because the corrupt Hanoverian system of government controlled its appointments. He felt that he owed his survival and religious culture to his fellow soldiers, especially his 'dear friend', Mark Bond from Durham, who died in the fighting. The men had organised their own religion, and the officers, while muttering about Oliver Cromwell, had for the most part let well alone – at least the converted soldiers fought well and gave little personal trouble.

Staniforth worked through his crisis until, in 1744, alone on guard duty at midnight:

I knelt down, and determined not to rise, but to continue crying and wrestling with God, till he had mercy on me. How long I was in that agony I cannot tell: but as I looked up to heaven, I saw the clouds open exceeding bright, and I saw Jesus hanging on the cross. At the same time these words were applied to my heart, 'Thy sins are forgiven thee.' My chains fell off, my heart was free.[32]

Here one has, in quick succession, Jacob wrestling with the angel, Stephen's vision 'of the heavens opened and the Son of Man standing on the right hand of God', and then the climax of the hymn Charles Wesley wrote immediately after his conversion in 1738, and which was based on Peter's angel-assisted escape from prison. The Wesleyan circle was complete.

The soldiers stand out among the early preachers as men living in a hard world of their own and reshaping it through the power of imagination. The only other passage which comes up to this in the Wesleyan canon is John Haime's description of his deliverance. Haime (1710–84) came from Shaftesbury in Dorset; he had a deeply depressive personality from which he suffered for twenty years, long after he left the Army and Wesley started to use him as a travelling preacher in 1747. He describes his original conversion, which happened in 1740, soon after he had enlisted, thus:

one Sunday, as I was going to church, I stood still like a condemned criminal before his judge, and said, 'Lord, what am I going to church for? I have nothing to bring or offer thee, but sin and a deceitful heart.' I had no sooner spoken, than my heart melted within me, and I cried earnestly to him for mercy. But suddenly something ran through my veins cold as ice. I was afraid to stay; and arose and left the room; but reflecting that God is above the devil, I went in again. I fell down before the Lord, with bitter cries and tears, till my strength failed me, and it was with difficulty that I could walk out of the room.

Then, as so often, in a moment of solitude, came the epiphany, in a kind of baptism: 'The next morning as I was going to water my horse, just as he entered the river, in a moment, I felt the love of God flowing into my soul. Instantly all pain and sorrow fled away.'[33]

Language was their element, imagination their way of thinking. The extraordinary depth-in-simplicity of early Wesleyan culture comes out again in the case of Thomas Mitchell (1726–85), another former soldier, born in Bingley in Yorkshire, whom the *Lives* officially described as having had 'slender abilities as a preacher' and 'a defective education'.[34] Not long before his death Mitchell contributed a short outline of his life and experience. This ended with a quotation from a hymn, the last stanza of which ran:

> In suffering be thy love my peace,
> In weakness be thy love my power;
> And when the storms of life shall cease,
> Jesus, in that important hour,
> In death, as life, be thou my guide,
> And save me, who for me has died.

This was not one of Charles Wesley's hymns, but John Wesley's translation of 'O Jesu Christ, mein schonstes Licht', which had been published by Paul Gerhardt (1607–76), the most notable hymnwriter of German Lutheranism, in 1653. The source lay even further back, in Jakob Arndt's *Paradiesgartlein* of 1612. It was sung at the eucharist held at the bedside of the dying Bengel in 1745. (J. A. Bengel (1687–1752) was a German Lutheran biblical scholar from whom John Wesley borrowed when writing on the New Testament.) Wesley translated the hymn in Savannah, Georgia, and it first appeared in England in 1739; a version was printed in the 1780 hymnbook as Hymn 362. In 1782 it had integrated itself into Mitchell's religious consciousness, and functioned naturally as a closing statement of faith. A culture had formed out of early experience, of war as well as of peace, and Mitchell, who in one sense was a man who did not know what to say, knew very well what had to be said.

After the death of Charles Wesley in 1788 and of John in 1791, the Wesleyan Connexion, now dominated by the itinerants, had about 57,000 members in England and Wales, just over 1,000 in Scotland, and almost 14,000 in Ireland. Between 1700 and the 1790s the population of England and Wales had risen from about five and a half million to about nine million. In the United States, now completely freed from the English Wesleyans both culturally and ecclesiastically, there were also about 57,000 members; there were a further 6,000 in the West Indies, Newfoundland and Nova Scotia.

The first generation of Wesleyanism acted as a destabilising force in England because part of a local community, generally rural but often urban in the Midlands and the North, reorganised itself, drawing away from the official lines of order, obedience, religion and morality, and provoking local resistance in doing so. We do not know why all this happened, except that the direct use of military force to impose socio-religious solutions was rapidly abandoned in England after 1700, and denominational institutions, above all the Church of England, lacked the state's power to enforce a single line. Simple religious unity – one state, one Church – became inconceivable. Wesleyan Methodism protested against this change in the status of the Establishment for a few years, but expanded at the same time because the Church of England no longer had the power to check it. When local people tried to eject or keep out Wesleyan preachers, the local magistrates in England found themselves politically obliged to protect the itinerants, even if they delayed doing so as long as they could.

The second wave of Wesleyanism, from the 1770s, paid the price for Wesley's steady emphasis on holiness and lost some momentum. Wesley had no new policy once circumstances forced him to admit the limitations of holiness. Wesleyan internal discussion was now about the denominational future, and was conducted as much by the itinerants as by their Anglican leaders. They argued about whether the Connexion should leave the established Church, whether the itinerants could either baptise or adminster holy communion, whether there was a Wesleyan form of ordination, and so on.

What happened in the growing new industrial centres – Bradford, Leeds, Liverpool and Birmingham, for instance – differed sharply. Here was the seed of a Wesleyan Methodism which in its turn would dominate a whole social area of new industry and urban culture, a space where Anglican institutions were thin on the ground in the eighteenth century. The episcopate was slow to recover the initiative, though this would be done by the end of the nineteenth century. There was no question of Methodism preventing revolution.[35] Revolution was never possible. The demands for political change in the 1780s were beaten off as the ruling elites quickly recovered their self-confidence after the disasters in the United States, and became more, rather than less, Tory. The confidence of the propertied classes remained enormous. Hanoverian governments never hesitated to use military force for secular and social purposes, when, for example, it was a question of putting down working-class movements. Force was only unavailable for religious purposes. It was applied to contain and break opposition from below, and it is interesting that 'Church and King' mobs could still be found in the 1790s. The American War of Independence was as decisive as the '45, because the English upper class reacted fiercely against defeat, instead of yielding to a sense of failure, as happened gradually after 1945 as the empire shrank. Wesley went with the flow of popular feeling, as he probably always had, combining his sense of what was in the popular and Protestant mind with High Church Tory political ideas about government and society.

One way of examining this is to study Charles Wesley's political verse, beginning with a look at his savage attacks on

John Wilkes, which show that enthusiasm for moral reform did not imply support for political reform, and also reflect the extreme tones of his royalism.

> And must the reformation spring
> From insults on a gracious King?
> Your rights licentious be maintained
> By sacred Majesty profaned?
> By poisoning a distracted nation
> By regicide or abdication?
> Sooner let Horne be dubbed a martyr
> And factious London lose her charter,
> Sooner be wicked Wilkes forgot,
> Or stinking like his memory rot
> And your whole mob, both low and high-born,
> Conclude your glorious course at Tyburn.[36]

Charles Wesley also wrote at length on the American War of Independence, praising those who supported the royal cause and denouncing both the American rebels and their English sympathisers. Typical of his output is a poem called 'Written on the Peace of 1783'. He began with a routine attack on the loyalty of the English political leadership:

> Allured and bought with Gallic gold
> Our statesmen have their country sold,
>   While, deaf to misery's cries,
> Innocent millions they compel
> Oppression's iron yoke to feel
>   Or fall a sacrifice . . .
>
> They force their country to receive
> A peace which only Hell could give,
>   Which deadly feuds creates,
> Murders and massacres and wars;
> A peace which loyalty abhors
>   And each true Briton hates.

This peace branded the English for ever, he said, over-whelmed them with infamy, and sank the British name. He

then justified his verdict by adding to the criticism of the
leadership an indictment of people in general:

> A peace which never could have been
> But as the punishment of sin,
> Of riot in excess,
> Of foul concupiscence and pride,
> Of crimes the great disdain to hide,
> Of general wickedness . . .

However unconcerned people might be as they rushed into
the pit, he commented, they could not escape the just reward
of their actions:

> When God awakes, the vengeful God,
> And inquisition makes for blood,
> Will he not call to mind
> Those pests of our afflicted race
> And turn them into their own place
> The murtherers of mankind?[37]

The righteous might have lost the war, but in the final judgement God would know who were the pests – the Americans,
their Dissenting supporters, and the traitors among the ruling
elite, politicians and generals who, in Charles's opinion, betrayed the American Anglicans who had resisted the impious
scheme of rebellion planned in Britain by patriot fiends, had
sacrificed their property for the Crown and who were refused,
as he believed, adequate compensation by the British government. At the end of all things, however, 'thy Church shall
see/a gracious difference made by Thee/in favour of thine
own'.[38]

Charles Wesley's difficulty in writing political verse is understandable. He had no gift for the kind of epigrammatic
punchline which was the great attraction of the genre. His mind
was soaked in the style and language of the Authorised Version,
with the result that in his political verse he sought to relate his

religious convictions to politics by means of moral judgements on individuals. He often employed unsuitable hymn metres, and, as the above passage illustrates, shifted from individual condemnation (John Wilkes, General Howe and Philip Shelburne, for example) to the Last Judgement, which would punish the politicians and spare the Wesleyans. It was not that he had no concept of society, but that he took for granted the divine approval of the existing order, that is, the settlement of 1688, which was not based on republican ideals. Reform, which meant change, was anathema.

These poems were not published in his lifetime, but Charles's opinions were well known inside the preaching fraternity, and they underline the problem which the Wesleyan leaders had in translating their apparent religious influence into a coherent political, as distinct from moral, form. George III's generals and politicians had not betrayed him, they were just incompetent. The English Dissenters had not fomented a rising in the American Colonies, but some Dissenting ministers were prepared to defend American independence. Francis Asbury threw the American Methodists behind the new republican state, and in doing so created a gap between American and British Methodism which has never been bridged.

4

Women in Wesleyanism

The importance of women in the development of early Wesleyanism has emerged in previous chapters, and a small group of personal testimonies, all written by Bristol women for Charles Wesley in 1742, survives to illustrate it.[1] It was actually George Whitefield, as a young, ordained Anglican minister turned itinerant preacher and fundraiser, who had first stimulated Bristol's Protestantism when he preached there in 1739, but he soon withdrew. At this point, with his agreement, two more Oxford-educated parsons who were well known to him, approaching forty years of age, unmarried, and, like Whitefield, had avoided the parochial ministry, were willing, without much reference to the existing parochial structure in Bristol, to involve themselves in the religious activities of those whom Whitefield had stirred up. Most of these people seem to have belonged to the small-business element of the city rather than to the very poor, though among the female adherents there were always widows, some of whom were not well off. From the beginning the Wesleys insisted on a tight personal relationship with those who listened to them. John Wesley's anxiety to have a kingdom of his own was crucial to the way in which the movement developed: there was to be no question of a brief preaching 'revival'. The new Wesleyan meetings separated those who attended them regularly from the rest of the city's religious culture. People found themselves living changed emotional lives; sometimes they enjoyed the fresh situations, sometimes they were upset.

The detailed inner working of the human personality in the grip of primary rather than official or elite religion had already begun to fascinate John and Charles Wesley, who constantly sought either written or oral self-description of their followers' experience. The individual religious histories from a small group of Bristol women throw a clear light on what was happening in Bristol during the first moments of the Wesleyan movement. The Wesleys tried to control and shape the underlying religious anxieties and expectations of those who came to hear them by making use of the secondary theological concepts of justification and sanctification: they wanted to know, for example, to what extent the Wesleyan's personal life would be changed by the gift of divine forgiveness. The women's accounts suggest that in their everyday lives they found it hard to come to terms with the resurfacing after conversion of passions such as anger, envy and jealousy, to say nothing of sex, but that they found compensating satisfaction in the belief that they had access to supernatural power, which protected them as individuals and excited in them ecstatic experience.

Much the same phenomena may be found in *The Lives of the Early Methodist Preachers*, where the masculine autobiographical accounts are the products of much longer and more sophisticated professional reflection. These were not written until the 1770s but some of them referred to the experience of the first Wesleyan generation. Comparison of the two shows that by the late 1760s the Wesleyan leaders had to ease the pressure of their idiosyncratic theology on daily life; they were responding more cautiously to the religious situation they had created. In the narratives of the 1770s the main role of Wesleyan women was defined by the full-time preachers; in the earlier narratives the women talked from their own point of view.

In their personal accounts of their religious life the Bristol women offered a public assertion about their private experience. They claimed an identity based on a direct relationship to a divine spirit which was perceived as masculine – that is, one finds no trace of a suggestion that the Holy Spirit might be feminine. They described their experience in language which had already been laid down for them by male authorities. This theological picture of divine-human interaction mattered less than the claim that these particular ordinary women were existentially taking part in the alleged divine-human transaction which the words specified. I do not mean that the women had been liberated in some twentieth-century sense; their personal identity might still be threatened in the long run, because the men who at this formative stage of Wesleyan history controlled the words which limited the women's behaviour were sometimes aiming at the virtual destruction of human personality.[2] To be theologically perfected one had to lose one's fallen self – not only selfishness but self could become a term of opprobrium. One had to acquire, or be given, 'the mind that was in Christ Jesus our Lord'.[3] From their own point of view, these Wesleyan women in Bristol in the 1740s were saying that they had the same internal religious experience as the men, even if they largely depended on men like John and Charles Wesley to interpret to them what was taking place.

There were competing identity-models, because one of the most sensible effects of the Reformation was the (albeit very slow) emergence of a more positive Christian attitude to sexual activity and marriage. In Protestantism Mary mattered, when she mattered at all, as mother, not virgin; or to put it another way, the supposed fact that Mary remained a virgin but became a mother did not recommend virginity to Protestants as a higher moral and religious state. The contrasting Roman Catholic attitudes survive: Pope John Paul II, for example, had canonised or beatified almost 300 people by 1997, but the list does not include a single woman who was not a virgin.[4] For Protestants, though, women could not imitate the way in which Mary became a mother; and both the value of the symbolism which her route to motherhood involved, and the roles for women which were often based on the slender New Testament stories, might reasonably be doubted. In the longer run this was the deepest divide cut by the Reformers, because baroque Catholicism turned increasingly to Mary as the focus of piety. In Protestant countries the importance of sexual asceticism declined, and the value of marriage was enhanced, without any strong link to the case of Mary at all. Even the interest in Christmas which developed in the early nineteenth century concentrated on the infant Jesus as the symbolic centre of a child festival, and relegated the mother of Jesus to a minor, or perhaps one should say normal, role.

This process of change was by no means complete in the eighteenth century. In John Wesley's personal case the evidence is clear. As a young man he thought it was 'unlawful for a priest to marry', grounding that persuasion on the (supposed) 'sense of the primitive church'. More importantly, as a result of reading what he called mystic authors, he concluded that 'marriage was the less perfect state . . . that there was some degree (at least) of taint upon the mind, necessarily attending the marriage-bed'.[5] The notion that sexual activity 'tainted' the mind certainly went back to the primitive Church, and Wesley overcame it – if he did overcome it to any great degree – only in the second half of his life. In 1749 he was at least prepared to say, on the authority of the Pauline Epistles, that 'the bed is undefiled, and no necessary hindrance to the highest perfection'.[6]

As far as the woman was concerned, the highest perfection still meant acceptance of the role of the obedient sex.

Samuel Richardson, for example, who as a novelist concentrated so much on the female consciousness (which he explored in Anglican theological as well as moral terms), seems to have regarded obedience, to the family and then to the husband, as the best because the safest mode of behaviour for women. This was partly because he saw that the social and economic inequality of the sexes provided women with only a weak position from which to reach for a more positive role, but also because female obedience still had the weight of theological opinion behind it. Three generations later, reasserting the English Roman Catholic tradition in the wake of the recent victory of conservative political forces over the French revolution, a victory which was also a setback for the kind of secular feminism associated with it, John Henry Newman was once again elaborating a feminine Christian character rooted in obedience and developed in humility. Humility and obedience led naturally (or supernaturally) to the abandonment of sexuality, so that ideally mothers would bear daughters who would become nuns, and the race would end to the glory of God. Christian theology clearly did not offer the most sympathetic context for the reconstruction of the feminine gender.

As far as the female converts of the Wesleys were concerned, liberation of a limited kind was certainly taking place in Bristol and Kingswood in the early 1740s. This is hard to define, but occasional, fragmentary states of ecstasy seem to have offered the basis for a new self-regard. Elizabeth Halfpenny, for example, had been drawn into the new current of religious activity by George Whitefield, and she was anxious to make clear to Charles Wesley that she had now broken completely with both Whitefield's Calvinism and John Cennick, who was moving away from the Wesleys in the equally improper (in Methodist eyes) direction of Moravianism.[7] She frankly recorded that she had been deeply attracted by John

Wesley himself, 'my soul never being at rest but when I was with him or hearing him talked of'.[8] She admitted that John Wesley had warned the women at Bristol against 'idolatrous love',[9] but she equally found her relationship with him a problem which she had not yet solved. Nevertheless, the dynamic relationship was with Charles Wesley, who had staggered her when he had said that in the next world 'we might be put on a level with Whores and Drunkards and Outward Sinners'.[10] It was Charles who had been preaching when she received the forgiveness of sins which would, technically, lift her away from the appalling prospect of sharing such company in hell. In addition, he had convinced her of the possibility of attaining perfection – she used the word herself – before she died. It was almost certainly when he was administering holy communion at Kingswood that 'in an instant [there] was brought to my view, by the eye of Faith, the form of a Tall Parson in his Surplice, his hair was White, and seemed to move on the ground with his back toward me, but he was soon Vanished'. The picture of God allowing Moses to see, not his face, but his back (Exodus 33: 19–21) seemed to haunt the eighteenth-century evangelical imagination, as can be seen in the more explicit case of Elizabeth Sayce (see below), and this may be another, rather low-key, example of the same scene. It must be remembered that English Protestants had no local images or paintings on which to draw for the content of visionary experiences. Halfpenny was now troubled by nothing (she declared) except fear that the Wesley brothers might die, and she signed herself 'your unworthy Servant and Daughter in the Lord'.[11]

Slight as the narrative is, it brings close an ordinary Wesleyan of the early years. First impressions suggest that Elizabeth Halfpenny, who had certainly been involved in religious groups since she had heard George Whitefield five

years before, had accepted the secondary theological formulae taught her by the Wesleys, and had enjoyed experiences
which she was encouraged to regard as confirming what she
had been told. She was aware of a sexual element in what was
going on, but did not think this was out of her control. She
does not seem, to use Felicity Nussbaum's expression, to reject the dependent character which men were imposing on her.
There is a further clue, however, to her outlook. Halfpenny
wrote that her business called her among 'fashionable people
of the world',[12] who tried to persuade her not to listen to the
Wesleyan preachers.[13] She was almost certainly unmarried,
supporting herself in one of the trades which supplied the
needs of the fashionable, or at any rate some of the better-
off, people in Bristol. Her situation, it may be supposed, was
vulnerable, and in the primary religious tradition she turned
first to Whitefield, then to the Wesleys, as sources of supporting power. She had accepted the support which her religious
adventures seemed to provide. Although this clearly meant a
high degree of dependence on the Wesleys at the time when
Halfpenny was writing, her emotional relationship with them
formed only part of what was happening.

Some of these themes are repeated in the case of Elizabeth
Sayce.[14] Here again the first contacts had been with Whitefield,
and she reacted as Halfpenny did to Charles Wesley's saying
that 'we deserve to be damned . . . I thought I might be ex-
cepted, thinking that I was not so bad as a whore or a drunkard.'
Nevertheless, she came round to the view that she was wicked,
'in so much that when I went to bed, I feared I should be in Hell
before the morning. I was afraid to go to prayer for fear of the
Devil, who I thought was in every corner of the house . . .'[15]
Sayce's record makes the interplay between the primary ex-
ploitation of Christianity and the official religion very clear:
for her, to be stirred religiously legitimated a vivid fear of

active diabolical forces, so that when she began to doubt that she had been justified she talked about yielding to a reasoning devil. She expected to find that an external power had transformed her personality, so she was alarmed to find that she still became angry. Her religious moods swung sharply. After hearing John Wesley preach she felt 'as if I was flying on the wings of love up to my Saviour's breast'.[16] On the other hand, she was so affected at a sacramental service that the minister told her that this was a place for rejoicing, not mourning. Mourning meant turning the full force of despair against the self.

On another occasion Charles Wesley, working to what was with him a deliberate method, destroyed her confidence by asking her whether she were not troubled with self and pride, and this resulted in a night vision which (she said) humbled her to the dust. 'I became in his sight a dead dog. I saw that I was in his sight less than nothing and vanity; and as a beast of the field.' Her sense of rejection by Wesley had been transformed into a feeling of rejection by God himself. Once more the vision centred on seeing the back of God– 'so gracious a sight it was that I know not how to forget it'. In her statement she avowed that she was still unsettled, but (significantly) had been quickened and strengthened since John Wesley had returned to Bristol for a time.

Once again the picture is complicated. The Wesleyan official idea of religion involved submission to both supernatural and pastoral authority. Charles Wesley's characteristically abrupt criticism of Sayce combined the assertion of masculine power with an official understanding of the nature of the Anglican priesthood. Sayce tried hard to be obedient. Her vision – she does write specifically of 'my seeing the vision' – faithfully reflected the idea of self-abasement, and made her 'shout with joy . . . for the Lord Omnipotent's condescension in thus humbling himself to behold a sinful worm, even dust and ashes'.[17] At the same time she depended heavily on the two Wesleys, who attached much importance to establishing control over the behaviour of their followers. This explains the steady attacks which John Wesley made on the theology of Whitefield and of the Moravians, attacks which spilled over into casting doubt on the basic morality of Calvinists and Moravians, so that the argument became that they could not be morally right because they were theologically wrong. He dismissed the adoring trust of the moderate Calvinist that God had numbered his soul among the elect as fatalism. Wesleyan women would not be drawn in such a dangerous direction.

Yet the subordination of women in a tightly ordered religious community which reflected the Anglican past was not the whole story. Primary religion is more individualistic than this, and it is not surprising, therefore, that women were not always content with a simple acceptance of masculine preferences. Visions, whether orthodox or eccentric in content, had never vanished from the Protestant culture, and when these women had visions they claimed that they were as in touch with supernatural power as the men, much as Quaker women had done before them. They could not build as much on this as their Quaker predecessors had, though, because the Wesleys did not want their radical movement to break free from their ministerial authority. The women were not necessarily satisfied with what the Wesleys brought them. In the cases mentioned above both women felt that ecstasy and power came and went. Primary religious activity sought a certainty of power, and the freedom to use it, but no theory of prayer which was offered to the women could guarantee prayer's success in a given situation.

There are two more cases which we can consider at this point, those of Naomi Thomas and Mary Thomas (who do not seem to have been related). Naomi Thomas, about whom nothing else is known for certain, heard Whitefield before she heard the Wesleys, but although she was frequently moved by the preaching it is far from clear that there had been any fundamental change in her life or behaviour. The following passage is typical:

I went on in this uncomfortable manner, dead, dull and weary of my self, and did not care whether I came to hear the word or no; but the last time you [Charles] came from Wales, I heard you expound, when the Lord manifested himself to me again. But I sometime after grew slack, and gave way to my corrupt and deceitful heart.[18]

She concluded: 'although I am now in the dark, but yet I know the Lord has not wholly forsaken me'.[19] She was drawing heavily here on the biblical language used in the meetings in order to describe her personal condition, and one cannot help wondering whether this language, though eloquent in itself, really helped her to understand what her problems were. The words she had heard translated her existence back into questions about sin and obedience – that is, the words were being used to impose a particular form of piety, when what she wanted was a source of activity.

The time sequence of the narrative is far from clear, but the impression given is that she, like others, was in constant need of fresh stimulus, which the Wesleys gave them, persuading them for the moment to believe that they would find in the Wesleyan societies the power to transform themselves for which they were looking. Whenever the Wesleys moved elsewhere, as they constantly did, what Naomi Thomas called deadness and darkness easily returned. In her case dependence and obedience were less sustained than in the two previous instances; she liked the feelings generated in the Wesleyan meetings, but found that as far as she was concerned nothing followed from them.

Her experience resembled that of Mary Thomas, who probably died in 1745, aged about sixty. She too, had, heard Whitefield before she heard John Wesley, who convinced her that although she did not swear or get drunk, 'I was a devil'. Her conviction of sin went on for some time and then 'Last St James fair was twelve month you [Charles] ordered the Society to come and speak with you . . . I came as I was and you asked me if I was justified and I said no. You told me I was in a state of damnation which words pierced my heart though it were what I had heard many times.'[20] She had since, she said, been justified, but reported that she was in this joy for about a fortnight, but then fell into the devil's snare again when she heard two young women telling each other what agony they had been in before they received forgiveness, and that those who did not feel such agony and cry out in the meeting were deceiving themselves in believing that they were saved. 'I had not been taken in such a manner,' Thomas commented drily. John Wesley had since revived her confidence, but even so 'I have not now such joy as I had.'[21]

Both these women seem strung out between their basic problems, of which we know no details; fear, which included a Wesleyan-strengthened fear of hell; and their present inability to handle their situation, probably because they are relying on a succession of emotional states to offer them a solution. It is possible that the greater emphasis which Wesleyanism put on primary religion had drawn Mary Thomas away from a conventional Anglicanism. At one point in her account she recalled how she had been brought up as a child to know the Lord, and this would have been before 1700. If (though this is hypothetical) she were the Molly Thomas who died in Bristol in 1745, the important words in the report which was sent to John Wesley were that 'she was always constant in the use of all the means, and behaved well both at home and abroad'.[22] The pointblank condemnation of the individual's existing personality, the insistence that only a direct experience of divine approval could stand between the individual and divine rejection – an approach which half-consciously played on the fear of inimical spiritual powers which was inherent in primary religion – was a technique Charles Wesley especially favoured and John supported, but it did not always strike the target. It should not be assumed that the mercurial Charles Wesley always assessed his contacts correctly.

The women's testimonies therefore tell us something about the mental universe they inhabited, and the Wesleys penetrated. The early followers had to believe (but, as Mary Thomas's case suggests, at times had great difficulty in believing) that they, personally and individually, were as threatened with perpetual damnation as were whores and drunkards. These seem to have been among the favourite examples, and their use left its mark, for some of the new Wesleyans resented the comparison, knowing that they did not behave in a way that merited it. Primary religion was not unaccustomed to the concept of a God who could be offended and repulsed, who did not always care to make nice distinctions between one kind of sinner and another, and who might reject one altogether and punish indefinitely. Official Christianity possessed both a devil and a hell, unrelieved in the Protestant case by the chances of a purgatory; one side of primary religion retained the images of maleficent spirits which could be appeased, even manipulated. The depth of the fear which sometimes gripped people is not to be doubted.

On the secondary theological level the Wesleys taught that one could be saved from these dangers by faith in Christ, a faith given firmer definition by the constant use of the verbal ikon of Jesus wounded, bleeding and dying, an image with which people were encouraged to identify themselves, though in practice in these years when Wesleyans had visions they were as likely to be of the Father as of the Son. Significantly, the women who had visions were usually tentative in trying to interpret them, as though the visions lacked a clear meaning for them. They asserted themselves in describing their visions, but they did not claim prophetic power. No class of shamans emerged, however strange the behaviour of individuals might be. In the class and band meetings where the women could become subordinate leaders, the stronger personalities slipped into a pastoral role.[23] The Wesleys did not encourage them to look back at the previous century or at the traditions of the Society of Friends to find precedents for their situation, whether as visionaries, prophets or leaders.

On the primary level people were happy to find ways of repelling evil supernatural forces. However, they often identified having faith with their experiences of possession or ecstasy, which happened sometimes when they were by themselves, but also in moments of intense collective excitement in the meetings of the society. When Elizabeth Sayce was asked about her experience of the witness of the Spirit, for example, she recalled the time 'at which we were all affected, so much that we were all one mighty blaze of the fire of love, God being in the midst of us as in the holy place of Sinai'.[24] Such experiences were important, because if they were really supernatural, believers might hope to find such power available in their everyday circumstances. The great number of hymns which Charles Wesley wrote in the first person singular helped to reinforce the individual's sense of living at the centre of a field of forces, and the Wesleyan hymnbooks acted as an Arminian alternative to the Calvinism of John Bunyan's equally self-centred *Grace Abounding*.

When the Wesleys stoked up the meeting into 'one mighty blaze', they were seeking to apply the theological idea of justification to people like Mary Thomas. The idea was not a simple one. The American scholar Norman Fiering once wrote that:

the seeker of redemption must adopt the paradoxical belief that he can change himself by the passive action of assuming responsibility or guilt (what the Puritans called conviction of self) . . . [the modern patient] and the seeker must accept that they are justly suffering for who they are by admitting in the end that the most despised elements in their personalities are, in effect, the product of deliberate choice as well as being at the same time the product of outside forces. By this process of humiliation and remorse, health and salvation are gained.[25]

This is well put, but it can be argued that this was neither quite what the Wesleys were saying nor quite what the early Wesleyans were doing. If Wesley's explanatory system was correct, the cultivated passivity of the personality would become the scene of divine activity, and the ecstatic experiences which sometimes followed related as much to a release from fear as to remorse. They bestowed a temporary sense of well-being. After all, once an individual had allowed the setting up of the damnation trauma, he or she expected to be released from it, and the relief could be identified with the idea of justification. What was not so easy was to set up the perfection process, the second stage of Wesleyan spiritual empowerment, so that it convinced the eighteenth-century spectator of Wesleyanism, for whom perfection was either nonsense or a kind of trap.

It is these early Wesleyans, expected to understand and conform to radical, theologically phrased demands which seemed to go far beyond the hopes and fears of primary religious energy, who remain interesting, not the hereditary Wesleyans of later generations. What John and Charles Wesley were doing in the 1740s was making closer contact with that general mythmaking capacity of the human imagination which seeks (in one of its modes) to use images to give a coherent account of direct human contact with sources of supernatural power. The effect of the first preaching was not an evangelical revival, though the possibility of something like one consciously occupied Wesley's mind, but a rediscovery of primary religious energies which were not, at that particular period, acting through official channels. Official religion, the established Anglican context from which many of the members of the first societies came, might be described as a metaphysics of order, offering grounds for obedience, social rather than personal, but also supporting a turn towards some form of private mysticism. Official Anglicanism was never as spiritually dead as the Wesleys said it was, or as Catholic historians have assumed it must have been, not being Catholic. There were whole aspects of Hanoverian Anglicanism which the Wesleys never fully understood. In the long run John Wesley made an orthodoxy of his own system, while asserting that this was the true system of orthodoxy. For him – but not for Charles, who reacted against lay initiatives in religion – the structure of Wesleyanism became more important than order in either the English Church or in English society.

In the 1740s Wesley's encounter with the mythmaking powers of the imagination galvanised individuals rather than the Anglican system itself. Wesleyanism competed with Anglicanism at ground level, but it had little effect on institutions which turned out to be much more rooted in English society than its critics hoped. John Wesley had thought of religion – as did another would-be reformer of the Church of England, John Henry Newman, in the 1830s – as a matter of finding out the verbal formulae of the true gospel and then applying them through language (preaching) in the power of a divine Spirit. Wesley himself needed an external authority, and cherished the notion of a definitive biblical religion all his life, polishing and repolishing it, but his experience of primary religion in the Wesleyan societies, and his psychological need to dominate the beliefs and actions of other people, made him concentrate on the order of what in effect was a gathered church. Once he had felt, in a Protestant context, the primary demands for ecstasy, healing, protection, self-belief and so forth working through those who listened to him, he never entirely escaped from the pressure to construct a new Wesleyan myth.[26]

The Wesleyan women members of the 1740s lived out an unrepeatable situation. They had to try to interpret their experience, and they did so largely on lines laid down by the Wesleys, lines which isolated them from what had happened before, especially what had happened in the seventeenth century. They had an opportunity to shape their lives, modifying the religious attitudes in which they had been brought up in terms of what they now encountered in the company of the Wesleys. Chance also played a part, because John Wesley might not have accepted Whitefield's invitation to take over in Bristol and might not have located there as firmly as he and his brother actually did. Both of them were strongly drawn to London, and both of them were to die there. The women faced a group of aggressive men – George Whitefield, the two Wesleys, the brilliant Moravian leader John Cennick and the Welsh Calvinist preacher Howell Harris, who was Whitefield's real successor in the West – all of them religious rhetoricians, for the most part ordained and socially superior, well equipped to compel emotional and intellectual surrender.

One suspects that many of these women in Bristol were initially looking for increased personal freedom and a moderate degree of happiness, and found it hard to compress their behaviour into the self-rejecting pattern of sin and justification demanded by the preachers. In these brief records they can be seen having to cope with their daily lives at the same time as coping with passionate demands that they live in accordance with the will of men who were expounding an invasive, unfamiliar style of Protestantism. Wesley's 'Arminianism', after all, was drawn from a seventeenth-century Dutch secondary theology which left men and women uncertain about their final salvation. Wesley contradicted the predestinatory Calvinism of Dissent and the evangelical Anglicans, threw his followers back on what he called their faith, and expected them to cope with the impact of dramatic ecstasy and nagging anxiety. It is hardly surprising that these women can sound bewildered.

In the second generation, from the 1760s on, the professionals would impose a more clearly defined ministerial leadership in place of the early improvisations, and would control the women more effectively. But it is an exaggeration to talk of the Wesleyan movement as lay, as Professor W. R. Ward has done.[27] The male professionals were constantly there, defining, driving, permitting, denying, taking the praise and often avoiding the blame. And the itinerants, placed at first in a second and lower rank of authority, quickly evolved into a full-time professional group which reinforced the will of the small group of leaders.

So it was that in the Bristol area in the 1740s the women found themselves part of a small, new, expanding religious community which used religious celebration and excitement as a means of defining itself and becoming a countervailing force in a city whose religious affiliations were as much Dissenting as Anglican. Early Wesleyanism provided them with a limited area of service as leaders of the female classes, and much greater prominence in the societies than most of them would have known in the Anglican parishes of the time. They were not, on the other hand, supposed to prophesy, or to indulge in criticism of the hierarchical structure of eighteenth-century England. Early Wesleyanism did not fully repeat the experience of the Society of Friends, which in George Fox's hands, and in potentially revolutionary times, had offered women a much more equal role than this. Wesley's late, unsuccessful marriage was not the religious equivalent of Fox's relationship with Margaret Fell.

Wesley denounced individuals, not institutions. Women who joined the early Wesleyan societies benefited from the temporary tumult of a unique religious situation, but Zion naturally failed to materialise and in the second generation the women found Wesleyanism more and more patriarchal. As time went on John Wesley allowed a very small number of women to preach, but there was never any question of their itinerating, or, in the last years of Wesley's life, when the issue of status had become the bitter core of Wesleyan politics, of their being ordained, as some of the men were. The majority of the male itinerants disliked women preachers as powerful competitors, and stopped the practice altogether once John Wesley was dead. The gradual change in the position of women in the eighteenth-century Wesleyan Connexion resembled the way in which women had at first played a prominent, often public part in the piety and politics of seventeenth-century Quakerism, but found themselves politely confined to domestic piety by the beginning of the eighteenth century. As a result, the Wesleyan movement was very gradually pushed towards Dissent and marginalised. The failure to make more generous use of women partly explains why Wesleyanism had lost its unity by the 1840s.

We know nothing more for certain about the women who wrote these short accounts of their religious lives for Charles Wesley in 1742. We do not know what difference Wesleyanism finally made to them. We do, however, have a more elaborate account of the impact of early Wesleyanism, and of the environment in which it flourished, on one particular woman. It comes, not quite directly, from Grace Murray, a woman with whom John Wesley was closely associated in the later 1740s, and whom he might have married, though this would have required his overcoming the manipulative interference of Charles. Her account of her religious experiences up to 1749 was recorded by John Wesley at the climax of their relationship, when she was thirty-three and he was about forty-six, and the text bears traces of editing by him. Wesley kept the account, which has survived, and no one has ever disputed the basic authority of the available text, as coming from Grace Murray herself as well as from him.[28] The document gives an excellent picture of the primary religious world which the Wesleys had penetrated, and the results of the encounter.

Grace Murray was born to Anglican parents in Newcastle upon Tyne in 1716. She left the city when she was eighteen in order to evade her father's wish that she marry, and joined her sister in London, where she was in service for a time. In 1736 she married a seaman, Alexander Murray; when he returned to sea she went back to Newcastle, pregnant, but suffered a miscarriage. She was in London again, and by now a mother, by 1739, when her husband hindered her from hearing George Whitefield. Within weeks Murray went back to sea, and two weeks later her child died. 'As I looked at her laid out upon the table, the thoughts of death seized strongly upon me. This was followed by a strange lowness of spirits, without any intermission.'[29]

A young woman asked her to go and hear Whitefield on Blackheath, and with her husband away she did so. 'When [Whitefield] was gone away ... I was utterly disconsolate again. I wept much in secret, I walked up and down but could find no comfort. I spent much time in the Churchyard, reading the inscriptions on the tombstones, and crying over my child's grave.'[30] The same young woman asked her to hear John Wesley, who preached in Moorfields on 9 September 1739. She was deeply affected, though not converted, but when he preached his last sermon at the Fetter Lane chapel before going to Bristol, 'as I stept off the bench in order to go home, suddenly I was struck down and fell to the ground. I felt as if my heart was bound round with an iron girdle; I knew myself to be a lost, damned sinner . . . Thus I continued for half an hour.'[31] She seems to have understood her evident depression, which was related to losing two children and the frequent long absences of her husband, in religious terms, and she was actually converted on 8 October 1739, in her own house, when Maria Price, probably the young woman who had originally taken her to hear Whitefield's and Wesley's preaching, was reading to her from Romans 5, 'being therefore justified by faith'.

Wesleyanism clearly operated at times as a sisterhood which helped women to cope with existence. Grace Murray was living in London, miles away from a family from which she had half broken, and could not rely on the close network which would normally have supported her. The emotions released by the preaching of Whitefield and Wesley, feelings which she summed up in the image of the 'lost, damned sinner', corresponded to her belief that her misfortunes, and especially the loss of her two children, pointed to some omission, failure or actual offence on her part which must somehow be made good before her depression would be lifted.

Grace Murray was not then a member of the Wesleyan society and did not become one until the following year, when she was admitted by Charles Wesley. In the meantime, she had a vision of 'God the Father looking upon me through his Son, as if I had never committed any sin. I saw the Son

as one with the Father, and yet distinct from Him.'[32] This
was a sound, orthodox vision, which happened when she was
alone and making her bed, and which she partly described in
words she had been taught. What mattered, however, were
the words 'as if I had never committed any sin'. She had had
two griefs, and become depressed; neither her family nor her
husband was available to help her, and whatever experiences
she now had were at one level a way of putting aside for the
time being the misery and guilt she had accumulated, and at
another level a way of recovering the favour of supernatural
powers which she had somehow set against her. The High
God was now on her side. These events were being recorded
after an interval of eight or nine years, however, and they were
transmitted through John Wesley: they were therefore twice
edited, and their significance should not be pressed too far.

Despite these religious experiences Grace Murray became
ill again after her husband's return from his voyage. She had a
third pregnancy in May 1741 but again it seems to have ended
in tragedy. Her husband sailed to Virginia, and in May 1742
she had a premonitory dream.

I was one night just laid down, when I felt a weight come upon my
feet. I thought the cat had come upon me and strove to push her off.
Presently I felt it rising higher and higher by my side, till it seemed
to lie by me at the full length of a man. I felt an awe, but no fear,
praying continually and knowing I was in the hands of God. After a
few minutes it rolled off and fell upon the ground. I fell asleep and
dreamed I saw my husband lying in his coffin. I cried and asked, 'Will
you not speak to me?' He just lifted up his eyes and shut them again.
When I waked I was convinced my husband was dead. But I was so
filled with God, that at this time nothing could disturb or interrupt my
happiness in him.[33]

The account of the dream has the clarity of frequent telling
and of Wesley's probable editing. Grace Murray's claim that

she felt no fear in the first part of the dream may have been intended to ward off any suggestion that her night visitant was diabolical. The premonition, which expressed a natural anxiety in the circumstances, was fulfilled: in October 1742 she learnt that her husband had been drowned. At that point she collapsed: 'For a week I continued with only intervals of sense; nor did I ever recover the memory I had before.'[34] In addition, she had lost, she said, her 'clear intercourse with God . . . [her] power to behold him with open face'.[35] In terms of primary religion she needed healing and divine intervention, yet neither was forthcoming for the moment.

As a young widow her only economic solution was to marry again, but when she returned to Newcastle and evidently thought of marrying a local Wesleyan, John Brydon, whom she claimed to have converted, John Wesley seems to have intervened to separate them, sending her away into the country. This was characteristic behaviour on Wesley's part, in the sense that he was always confident of his ability to take moral and life decisions for other people, though not many were as amenable as Grace Murray to his direction. When Wesley went to London in April 1743 she followed him; she had begun to identify her social and personal salvation with him. In London she fell ill again, but said that she was assured by God that she would be saved at last, even though 'it will be as by fire'. In the autumn of 1743 she had to return to Newcastle; from then until Christmas 1744 she was extremely depressed but also an active Wesleyan. At no point in the narrative thus far did Wesley leave any sign in the manuscript version that he disagreed with her description of these past events.

Her wretched existence during the 1740s throws light on the adverse pictures which some critics of Wesleyanism offered in the early period. They interpreted Wesleyanism in secular terms, suggesting that it first generated symptoms of despair, then claimed to remove them by supernatural means. Early eighteenth-century doctors such as George Cheyne (1671–1743) had already, before Whitefield and the Wesleys came on the scene, diagnosed a personality disorder:

a kind of melancholy, which is called religious, because it is conversant about matters of religion, although often the persons so distempered have little solid piety. And this is merely a bodily disease . . . the mind turns to religion for consolation and peace, but as the person is in a very imperfect and unmortified state, not duly instructed and disciplined, and ignorant how to govern himself, there ensues fluctuation and indocility, scrupulosity, horror and despair.[36]

This passage comes from Cheyne's *Treatise on Health and Long Life*, of which the sixth edition appeared in 1725. Wesley was acquainted with this book, and also with *The English Malady*, which Cheyne published in 1733. Cheyne argued that the state of the body influenced the state of the mind, a proposition which John Wesley was prepared to accept when it suited him, while retaining his primary belief that God sometimes permitted evil spirits to inflict diseases for spiritual reasons.

In Grace Murray's case the symptoms of depression became acute. On one occasion, when she was out by herself, she 'felt a cloud fall in a moment, as it were, on my body as well as soul'.[37] She was tempted to suicide. An unspeakable horror fell upon her, that God had forgotten her and given her up to the devil. She heard Thomas Maxfield preach against Calvinism, and identified with a Calvinist woman who had believed she had been created in order to be damned and had died in deep despair. Stories of this type had been a familiar part of anti-Calvinist propaganda since the sixteenth century. Grace Murray said that she was sometimes so afraid that she thought she was dropping into hell. She described how she 'felt as if one had begun at the crown of my head and flayed off

my skin, yea, my flesh and all, to the very soles of my feet'.[38]
She grew very thin, fasting severely during the Lent of 1744,
and again thinking briefly of suicide.

One reason for her fasting was 'that I might destroy whatever it was, whereby I had been a snare to men; that I might
never hurt any man more'.[39] This sounds like the familiar
religious attempt to reject one's sexuality. She seems also to
have meant that she had caused suffering to both Murray and
Brydon in the past; she does not link her condition directly to
her loss of three children. She seems at times to have been trying to feel guilty, that is, to bring her life story into line with the
Wesleyan account of the human condition. Her basic depression, however, was not caused by Wesleyanism: Wesleyanism
was the religious technique to which she turned to alleviate
her sufferings. She clung to the societies, though there was
also a personal element, in as much as she was attracted by
Wesley. This is a thread in the pattern already seen at work in
Bristol. How she explained to herself the threatening collapse
of her personality at the time (1744) is unknowable, because
the source is retrospective. In the narrative she swings between
the conviction that she had offended God the Father and the
belief that she was being punished because she had hurt men.
In such a patriarchal culture her immediate remedy was to
conciliate men.

This element of negotiation has to be borne in mind, but the
kind of response she was likely to have had from the Wesleys
at the earlier point can be seen in the narrative verse which
John Wesley wrote a few days after Grace Murray finally
married John Bennet, when Wesley was anxious to fit what
had happened into his normal assumption that he had a right
relationship with God. He explained her condition in 1744 to
his own satisfaction by writing:

> But oh what trials are in store
> For those whom God delights to bless
> Abandoned soon to Satan's power,
> Sifted as wheat, from the abyss
> The lowest deep she groaned aloud:
> Where is my Joy, my Hope, my God?
>
> In chains of horrid darkness bound,
> Torn by the dogs of hell she lay;
> By fear and sin encompassed round
> Anguish and pain and huge dismay.[40]

In these lines Wesley offered her a stock theological explanation of her condition: for the moment, God had allowed the devil to tempt her. She must respond by keeping the faith until God 'anew unvailed his face'. In the verse narrative Wesley actually attributed her eventual recovery – at the time it was only partial – to himself:

> To one, by ties peculiar joined,
> One only less beloved than God,
> 'Myself', she said, 'my soul, I owe,
> My guardian angel here below.'[41]

This was not the version of the matter which Grace Murray herself gave in her own narrative, where she categorically ascribed her recovery to a conversation with a Mr Briggs, one of Wesley's itinerants, who had arrived in Newcastle from London at Christmas in 1744. She told Briggs that after she had refused to marry the young man Brydon, he had, in her view, become increasingly sinful, and that she had partly accounted for her own anxiety and depression by telling herself that she would have to answer for his loss of faith. Briggs convinced her that she had nothing to fear. She was immensely relieved: 'My doubt concerning the Sins of Jno. Brydon being imputed to me, was now removed, and the horrible dread was taken away.'[42]

Her anxiety did not in fact entirely disappear, but transferred itself to the state of the nation, which she felt was about to suffer the wrath of God in punishment for its iniquities. 'As I was one morning alone, a dread fell upon me, as if we were all ready to be destroyed. I thought the Papists were just going to swallow us up.'[43] When the Jacobite rebellion broke out in August 1745, it 'was no surprise to *me*'.[44]

In December 1745 John Wesley put her in charge of the so-called Orphan House (it was a kind of hostel) in Newcastle, and the position of responsibility clearly gave her confidence. There she nursed itinerants who were taken ill, including Thomas Westall, at that time about thirty years old, and she tells a story of how, in the autumn of 1746, she and Westall:

> went up together one night to the [roof]leads. As we were sitting, he told me, how the devil had tormented him at Bristol . . . and immediately he cried out, 'He is not far from us now.' I said, 'I feel him near, but God is nearer than him.' We came down into the kitchen and began to sing, but we knew not how to leave off. We continued singing and praying one after the other, and did not rise until it was past 12 a clock. The same Spirit of Prayer was upon us the next day and so every day until the following Thursday: so that we could scarce do anything but pray day and night, and continued therein twice, till past two in the Morning.

I think that at this point Grace Murray had gone beyond the role of the intermittently depressed innocent which she sometimes adopted: the devil and sex were not far apart on the roofleads. She could not prevent herself from attracting men, or from discussing her relationships with her acquaintances. As it was, she and Westall, thoroughly in the toils, fasted and led the bands in similar exercises. 'Elizabeth Boomer was not at the Bands, being confined in her own house. But she did not thereby lose her share of the blessing. She saw (as she afterwards said) the glory of the Lord at that very hour,

resting upon the house and was filled in an unusual manner with peace and joy in the Holy Ghost.' On the Saturday
three women were converted, including a Mrs Armstrong
(who 'soon after died in peace') and Grace Murray's mother.
The narrative continues: 'After Prayer, we went to breakfast.
In the midst of which I cried out, "I see Mr. C. W. He is
not far off." And in a few minutes after, Mr. W[esley] and
Mr. Perr[one]t came to the gate.'[45]

At this point it is worth summarising Grace Murray's account. Her early married life was difficult, because she lost
two children and suffered what may have been postnatal depression. Her seaman husband was away for long periods and
she had lost touch with the support of her family network by
moving south to London; she was easily persuaded to turn
to Whitefield, then to the Wesleys, for what has to be seen
as healing. The men seem to have increased a sense of guilt
she already had at the heart of her depression and whose exact cause is not clear: she does not herself directly connect
her illness with the loss of her children. She collapsed in one
of John Wesley's services. The sense of being healed finally
developed not in one of the Wesleyan society meetings but
when she was working in her house, where she had a vision of
God the Father, who accepted her. Her misfortunes continued, however, for she lost a third child, and when her husband
was at sea again she had a highly dramatic dream in which she
believed she foresaw his death. When she learnt that he had
indeed been drowned, she collapsed once more.[46]

At this stage her solution would have been to remarry, and
the fact that John Wesley himself prevented her from doing
so is a turning-point in the story. It is clear that he explained
her renewed depression by suggesting that God had given her
over to the devil for a period of testing, provided her with
work, and quietly fed her increasing emotional dependence

on him. She gradually recovered, and had another vivid but triumphant encounter with the devil in the Newcastle Orphan House.

Wesley entirely accepted her translation of her situation into religious terms: there can be no question in this relationship of drawing distinctions between Grace Murray's popular culture and Wesley's official or elite culture. He accepted the narrative of a strange battle with evil forces which lurked around the rooftops and pursued one down into the kitchen where one prayed and fasted and sang and sang until a feeling of ecstatic deliverance supervened. Caution is required here, though, for despite its apparent spontaneity this was also a ritual, like the communal or congregational casting out of the devil in twentieth-century Brazilian Pentecostalist services, which seem to combine in a similar fashion both passion and familiarity with the procedure.[47] For women the expected role was one of submission, combining the maternal presence in the home with a limited freedom, under the masculine pastorate, in the societies. Wesley's later marriage with Mrs Vazeille failed completely because, older than Grace Murray and with a child and money of her own, she was not prepared to accept Wesley's definition of submission.

Grace Murray's attraction for Wesley lay in her perceived willingness to submit. In his verse narrative he represented himself as having understood what was going on within her:

> From heaven the grateful ardour came
> Pure from the dross of low desires;
> Well-pleased I marked the guiltless flame;
> Nor dared to damp the sacred fire.[48]

He distinguished her from other Wesleyan women in the North-East by taking her with him not only through the country societies surrounding Newcastle but also to Ireland in the spring of 1748. In the verse narrative he described her as expressing astonishment when he suggested that she was help prepared for him in heaven, and that their souls had been 'joined above / In lasting bonds of sacred love':

> Can God, beyond my utmost wish
> Thus lift his worthless handmaid up?
> This only could my soul desire:
> This only (had I dared) require.

This was Wesley's own language, and he went on to describe their relationship.

> Companions now in weal and woe
> No power on earth could us divide;
> Nor summer's heat nor wintry snow
> Could tear my partner from my side;
> Nor toil, nor weariness nor pain,
> Nor horrors of the angry main.

> Oft (though as yet the nuptial tie
> Was not) clasping her hand in mine,
> What force, she said, beneath the sky,
> Can now our well-knit souls disjoin?
> With thee I'd go to India's coast,
> To worlds in distant ocean lost.[49]

What Grace Murray actually said or did at this particular time will never be known, but Wesley's intention in these two stanzas was to put her in the wrong. The verse narrative provides no transition between this apparent union and the moment when 'the tempest' tore Grace from his 'inly-bleeding heart'. The unsearchable Lord had changed the situation and Wesley, 'a deeply-humbled son', must accept the will of God. The final stanza, addressed to God as Father, should be read bearing in mind his later, but not that much later, marriage with Mrs Vazeille:

Teach me, from every pleasing snare
To keep the issues of my heart:
Be thou my love, my joy, my fear,
Thou my eternal portion art.
Be thou my never failing friend.
And love, O love me to the end.[50]

The verses offered no explanation for the collapse of his relationship with Grace Murray. God was made responsible: 'O why didst thou the Blessing send? Or why thus snatch away my Friend?' Wesley's prose narrative was much more specific, distributing the responsibility between his brother, Charles, who was equally hostile to Mrs Vazeille, and who probably resented anyone else having a close influence over John, and various women in the Wesleyan societies who objected to what they saw as a fundamental alteration in the structure of the movement, the emergence of a joint leadership.

This was not what Wesley had in mind, but, nevertheless, he defended the proposed marriage on the ground that Grace Murray was the perfect religious partner for him. He described her in terms of useful obedience. As a housekeeper (the level at which his argument began) 'she understands all that I want done', he argued; as a nurse she was just what his 'poor, shattered, enfeebled carcase now frequently stands in need of'; as a friend 'she watches over me both in body and soul – sympathizing with me and helping me in all'; and as a fellow-labourer (that is, as an itinerant evangelist) she was 'both teachable and reprovable'.[51] Moreover, she both could and would travel with him: it was a paramount point that the marriage should not interfere with his religious activities. There was of course the possibility that she might become a mother (in 1749 she was thirty-three and he was forty-six, and she did later have children with Bennet), but if so the children could be brought up at the residential school which he had established at Kingswood, near Bristol, and she was, he claimed, willing to agree with this. He insisted that she was crucified to the world, desiring nothing but God, dead to the desire of the flesh, to the desire of the eye, and the pride of life.

In his efforts to defend the proposed marriage on religious grounds, Wesley fell back (despite his protestations to the contrary) on the hyperbole which came easily to him:

And as to the fruits of her labours, I never yet heard or read of any woman so owned of God: so many have been convinced of sin by her private conversation; and so many have received remission of sins in her bands or classes or under her prayers. I particularly insist upon this. If ever I have a wife, she ought to be the most useful woman in the kingdom: not barely one, who probably may be so (I could not be content to run such a hazard) but one that undeniably is so. Now, shew me the woman in England, Wales or Ireland, who has already done so much good as G. M.. I will say more. Shew me one in all the English annals, whom God has employed in so high a degree? I might say in all the History of the Church, from the death of our Lord to this day. This is no hyperbole, but plain, demonstrable fact. And if it be, who is so proper to be my wife?[52]

This, for all the exaggeration, had its pathos, betraying the desperation of a man arguing against the majority, and trying at the same time to keep his desires within the frame of his religious assumptions. If he also talked in such terms – though there is no way of knowing how far he did – he was saying things which his sharpest critics would use to accuse him of putting Grace Murray before God. He himself quoted Jane Keith especially, a Scotswoman who hovered between Wesleyanism and Presbyterianism, finally settling for the latter. She had said: '1. That Mr W. was in love with G. M. beyond all sense and reason; 2. That he had shown this in the most public manner, and had avowed it to all the Society, and

3. That all the Town was in uproar, and all the societies ready to fly to pieces.'[53]

Perhaps the movement itself had come close to hysteria generated by success in the late 1740s, and too much talk about 'holiness' had been taken too seriously, not least when Charles Wesley, himself safely married, attacked his brother for changing his mind about the religious appropriateness of marriage for someone so committed and called by God to reviving Christianity. The new Wesleyan institution was certainly not working perfectly. Wesley himself had replied to Charles that he had modified his theological position, that 'St Paul [had] slowly and gradually awakened me out of my Mystic Dream',[54] and that he was satisfied that his marriage was theologically permissible. Nevertheless, he was stung by Jane Keith's accusation of what he summed up as inordinate affection for Grace Murray, and in the prose narrative, written after Grace Murray and Bennet had married, rejected the idea that he loved the woman more than God. Inordinate affection, he said, led one away from God, whereas his feelings for Grace Murray had actually increased his passion for evangelism. He had never, he claimed, felt a minute's jealousy towards Bennet, nor a minute's resentment towards those 'who tore her from me', whereas inordinate affection would have produced such feelings.

The absolute denial was characteristic of Wesley's style. Moreover, he went on, excessive love made one uneasy in the absence of the loved one, 'whereas I never was uneasy, neither in parting, nor after it; no more than if she had been a common person'. He may have remembered here that after his own marriage Charles Wesley had written to John to point out how cheerfully he was able to leave his new wife to resume itinerating. His final argument was simple: 'if I had had more regard for her I loved than for the work of God, I should now have gone on strait to Newcastle [and tried to keep Grace Murray] and not back to Whitehaven. I knew this was giving up all: but I knew God called: and therefore, on Frid.29, set out.'[55] He went on to record 'great heaviness', relieved by preaching and prayer. He even spoke of having 'accepted the just punishment of my manifold unfaithfulness and unfruit-fulness, and therefore could not complain'.[56] He was trying hard to argue that he was right in believing that Providence had decided the issue, and that he himself was to blame in what had happened, and was being punished. He seemed to take the accusation of inordinate affection to himself. At this stage he did not know whether Grace Murray's marriage to Bennet had taken place.

All these religious exercises did not quite convince him of the righteousness of Providence. Just how close his religious temperament was to that of Grace Murray, and how important to early Wesleyanism was the primary religious impulse, then became clear. He recorded that:

we [that is, the Society, but especially Perronet] then poured out our hearts before God. And I was led, I know not how to ask, That if he saw good, he would show me what would be the end of these things, in dreams or visions of the night. I dreamed I saw a man bring out G. M., who told her, she was condemned to die: and that all things were now in readiness, for the execution of that sentence. She spoke not one word, nor showed any reluctance, but walked up with him to the place. The sentence was executed, without her stirring either hand or foot. I looked at her, till I saw her face turn black. Then I could not bear it, but went away. But I returned quickly, and desired she might be cut down. She was then laid upon a bed. I sat by mourning over her. She came to herself and began to speak, and I awaked.[57]

In the prose narrative Wesley made no comment which would enable readers to decide whether he thought God had answered him in this dream, and still less in what way he had been answered. This does not mean that he did not interpret the dream, or that he found no support in it, but the only clue to his reaction is that he continued to feel that Providence was in charge of his life. In fact, if one looks at what happened from Grace Murray's point of view, and ignores the religious terminology into which Wesley slipped after what he still saw as a disaster, the collapse of their relationship – which he explained, or perhaps accepted, as virtually a change of mind on the part of Providence – was probably caused by Grace Murray's own change of mind. When the struggle with his rival, John Bennet, was coming to a crisis in September 1749, Wesley noted: 'Yet I could not consent to her repeated request, to marry immediately.' He told her that before he could marry her it would be necessary to mollify Bennet, to procure Charles Wesley's consent, and to inform all the itinerants and their societies of his reasons for marrying. She said that she would not be willing to wait for more than a year, and he answered that perhaps less time would suffice.[58]

Put in this detailed way, John Wesley's proposals were far from simple. Grace Murray knew that neither Bennet nor Charles Wesley was likely to agree to the marriage, and she also knew that many articulate Wesleyan women were jealous of her influence on Wesley. He had made a major error of judgement in taking her with him to Ireland. Bennet was willing to marry her immediately; Wesley was prepared to negotiate for a marriage which might not in the end take place. She wanted and, in terms of the social context, needed to marry; she was no longer young, and marriage would solve, and did solve, her personal problems. Bennet, who figures unflatteringly in Wesley's narrative, was having a successful career as a travelling preacher but wanted to settle down in a single place with his own congregation. Always a stronger character than Wesley supposed, Grace Murray made her own decision, not least because Charles Wesley behaved as she had expected. No doubt she was prepared to be obedient to Bennet, but Wesleyanism, by freeing her from the numbing grip of her past, had changed the nature of that submission. Much more than before, she was her own woman.

John Wesley's heavily slanted narrative, intended to show that Grace Murray loved him rather than Bennet, gives a revealing account of the meeting of the Newcastle society in the hands of Charles. John believed that Charles had told the members that his brother had used his:

whole art and authority, to seduce another man's wife . . . all in the house (unless one or two that were instant in prayer) were set on fire, filled with anger and confusion and driven to their wits' end. S[ister] Proctor would leave the House immediately. John Whitford would preach with Mr. W. no more. Mat. Errington dreamed the house itself was all in flames (and most certainly it was). Another dreamer went a step further, and saw Mr. W, in hell-fire. Jane Keith was peremptory 'John W. is a child of the Devil'; coming near J. B[ennet] himself; whose repeated word was, 'If John W. is not damned, there is no God'.[59]

This was what other people told John Wesley had happened, not what he had heard himself. The speakers quoted often used religious references to express their feelings, but the report leaves the impression that their language was a sort of sanctified swearing. In general meetings of the society like this one, when the members acted as a cross between a court and a town-meeting, women were as free to give their opinions as men. This kind of local freedom apart, 'primitive Christianity' altered little in the patriarchal system which characterized Western churches.

If Wesley was aware that Wesleyanism had helped change women's perception of themselves, in line with what had been happening in the seventeenth century, he gave no sign of it. The Connexional structure as Wesley bequeathed it to the itinerants, through his formal creation of the Legal Hundred (a lawyer's concept which defined what Wesleyanism was in the eyes of the state), left no place for women in the direction of the movement at the national level. Women supplied an audience and offered hospitality; locally they might become spiritual counsellors, primarily for other women. There was no question of Wesleyan women having 'concerns', in the formal sense that Quaker women could claim that the Spirit had given them a specific mission or 'concern', which they were obliged to discharge, and which male Friends hesitated to question. Elizabeth Fry was more prominent than any Wesleyan woman in the early nineteenth century.

There was no apparent 'feminisation' of religion in late eighteenth-century Wesleyanism, because after Wesley's death in 1791 the male itinerants, buoyed up by the rapid expansion of the societies in the 1780s, and by Wesleyanism's independent success in what was now the United States, did not feel excessively dependent on the support of women. As the societies consolidated into a new variant of the chapel subculture which had been emerging in Dissent since the 1660s, women were allowed merely to extend their domestic role into that of a vast providing agency, which not only made tea and fed innumerable meetings, but raised large sums of money for the Connexion.

Anglican responses

The surprise with which so many Anglicans reacted to the emergence of a perfectionist group which claimed to be Anglican becomes more explicable when set against the changing cultural background of the late seventeenth and early eighteenth centuries. Thomas Hobbes (1588–1679) offers a natural starting-point, because he shocked his contemporaries, not by passionate religious aspiration, but by his thorough rejection of religious dogmatism, and his belief that the human mind worked best in sceptical isolation. Hobbes was too cautious to rule out the possibility of a written revelation, but he restricted the claims of theology that truth had already been divinely revealed. No supernatural intervention illuminated the minds of men and women to bestow wisdom from above: a stable, ordered society had to be maintained by absolute power. At his most sarcastic, Hobbes argued, in a discussion of 'separated essences':

theologians say that Faith, and Wisdom, and other Virtues are sometimes powred [sic] into a man, sometimes blown into him from Heaven; as if the Virtuous and their virtues could be asunder; and a great number of other things that serve to lessen the dependence of Subjects on the Sovereign Power of their Country. For who will endeavour to obey the laws, if he expect Obedience to be Powred or Blown into him?[1]

Hobbes crisply summarised how he thought the Protestant tradition viewed salvation. Christ 'did make that Sacrifice and

Oblation of himself, at his first coming, which God was pleased to require, for the Salvation at his Second Coming, of such as in the meantime should repent, and believe on him'.[2] 'Scripture', he held, 'was written to shew unto men the Kingdome of God, and to prepare their minds to be his obedient subjects, leaving the world and the philosophy thereof to the disputation of men, for the exercizing of their natural reason'. This section ended drily: 'so that I see nothing at all in the Scripture that requireth a belief, that Demoniacs were any other thing but Mad-Men'.[3]

The idea of holiness had little weight with Hobbes. He rejected the assertion that 'faith and sanctity are not to be attained by study and reason, but by supernatural inspiration'.[4] Faith and sanctity were indeed not very frequent, he commented, but 'they are not miracles, but brought to pass by education, discipline, correction and other natural ways by which God worketh them in his elect, as he thinketh fit'. Faith and obedience were both needed for salvation, but Hobbes argued that even in a 'Christian commonwealth we might be said to be justified when we plead our will, our endeavour to fulfil the law, and repent us of our failings, and God accepteth it for the performance itself'.[5] Professional theologians disliked this commonsense view of man-God relations.

Hobbes is relevant not because he had no predecessors – he presented a more brutal version of Montaigne – but because he showed that a humanised pattern of social behaviour might grow from the ruins left by the Civil War and a half-hearted Restoration. Moderate Anglicans in the following century might be horrified by what they considered Hobbes's atheism, but they sympathised with his psychological reading of salvation, whereas the Wesleyans fully believed that sometimes faith and wisdom could be blown into a man or woman from heaven. As for John Wesley himself, the scriptural text disarmed his mind, leaving him helpless in the presence of men and women convinced that both the Holy Spirit and evil spirits could overpower the human mind. Wesley was not stupid, but he was steeped in an inadequate tradition and found it hard to criticise what people told him and what they seemed to do and suffer.[6]

These conflicts influenced what has been called the Latitudinarian moral theology, against whose Walpolian form both Whitefield and the Wesleys reacted. An old cultural struggle simmered between an Augustinian-style despair of human nature, and a moderate Anglican, modernising faith which looked back to Erasmus and the Cambridge Platonists. In general, the Latitudinarians held that human beings could and should cooperate with God's grace because they retained some traces of the image of God in which they had been created: in theological terms, they did not suffer from total depravity. A modern defender of the Latitudinarians has conceded that:

the 'Restoration divines preached that doing good is a fundamental part of Christianity, that goodness is part of the great design of Christianity, and this was bound to mean the exaltation of charity, diligence, duties to self and neighbour, social virtues and public piety . . . but to conclude, as some have, that the Restoration churchmen were peddling a merely utilitarian system of ethics, and promoting it through an appeal to self-interest and prudence, is a bizarre and highly selective interpretation of their views.'[7]

Latitudinarians believed that God would save those who offered 'a faithful though imperfect obedience, an obedience suitable to man's natural infirmity and frailty, and proportionable to the assistance afforded to him'.[8]

This leads us, in a gentler, less purely Anglican vein to the further modernising ethical shift associated with the Earl of Shaftesbury (1671–1713) and Francis Hutcheson (1694–1746), a shift which concentrated on feeling, rather than on reason or intuition, as the source of morality. Just as one could improve one's taste in architecture, painting and sculpture on a Grand Tour, one could cultivate one's moral sense by trusting the guidance of an inner prompting on how to respond to experience. This ability to refine one's moral perceptions might operate in a theistic context, but not necessarily in a Christian context. The American scholar Norman Fiering argues that what Hutcheson was doing was secularising the Catholic and Protestant theories which had been generated by religious experience in the seventeenth century, and which had been employed by spiritual directors and pastors to mould and control through their own religious vocabulary what happened in the personalities of those who came to them for advice. He said:

Hutcheson's complex and discriminating sensations of shame, honour, virtue, vice, and compassion and beauty were secularised versions of the intuitive and essentially nonintellectual taste and relish, illumination and heart, holy affections and gracious dispositions of the saints. The difference was, of course, that Hutcheson did not regard supernatural intercession as the precondition of these.[9]

Hutcheson and Shaftesbury did not substitute one moral language for another – they had no intention of secularising the kinds of moral behaviour which the religious casuists extolled. They pointed to the sense of pleasure and balanced self-satisfaction which accompanied the knowledge that one had behaved in a moral manner. Enlightenment implied a clearing of the mind about the possibilities of human personality and human activity. Christian views of human nature were increasingly seen as a repulsive denial of the self and of the enlightened man's or woman's capacity to transform city and country, agriculture and industry, thought and letters.

Both George Whitefield and the Wesley brothers took a view of people's conduct to which not only the more sceptical,

but also most moderate Anglican writers responded with a firm
negation. The Wesleyans believed the majority of people
were hastening towards permanent punishment in hell. This
position underpinned John Wesley's answer to the open
attack by Edmund Gibson, bishop of London, on his Anglican
loyalty in 1747, when Gibson said that Wesley used highly un-
warrantable methods to prejudice people against the parish
clergy, and then to seduce their flocks from them.[10] Wesley
rejected the criticism, countering that in Moorfields, for example, there were 'ten thousand poor souls for whom Christ
died rushing headlong into hell', and that if, despite the efforts of the parochial minister, 'they are still in the broadway
of destruction' – and he personally had no doubt about their
destination – the Wesleyans were entitled to take a hand.[11] He
should be understood in eighteenth-century terms as referring to the governed rather than to the governing elements in
Hanoverian society when he talked about ten thousand souls,
but he did not exclude anyone. How he knew that they were
rushing headlong into hell, or that their forgiveness by God
depended on their having the chance to respond with faith to
Wesleyan preaching, is another question. In response, Gibson
was bound to doubt Wesley's authority.

Nor did Gibson accept Wesley's argument that it did not
matter whether or not the parish priest agreed with what the
Wesleyans wanted to preach. Wesley invariably took his own
decision as to whether to set up a Wesleyan society in an
Anglican parish. But the distinction between the would-be
evangelist, for whom an encounter with the local community
stimulated a picture of a mass of people spinning out of control
into damnation, and the local parson, who might well have
imagined his parish to contain a web of human relationships
whose inner meaning and final outcome remained hidden not
only from him but also from the individuals themselves, had

no appeal for the bishop of London. The evangelist's hope was that this imagined eternal crisis, controlled by a God in whom mercy struggled with justice, would mesh with local despair so that 'ten thousand poor souls' might find themselves swept, not into hell, but into ecstasy.

If one wants to understand the Anglican response to Wesleyanism clearly, John Wesley's *Journal* becomes a pivotal document, because the author regarded himself as an Anglican, whatever other Anglicans thought of his irregular behaviour. His case was more ambiguous than George Whitefield's, because the latter quickly reconciled himself to an independent existence in America, apart from his role in the Countess of Huntingdon's Connexion, a small but persistent English Congregationalist body. Whitefield's withdrawal from English conflicts did not mean that moderate Calvinism died out in the Establishment: in fact, more parochial clergy seem to have responded to its dark psychology than embraced the Wesleyan movement. It was Wesley's holiness movement which failed to take root in the Church of England. The negative Anglican response dated from the earliest days of organised Wesleyanism.

To understand this response, it is necessary to look at John Wesley's *Journal* for 1740, which covers a period of intense strain, when the first small group of Wesleyans detached themselves from the Moravians, with whom they had intermingled for about two years. On 23 July 1740 the London Wesleyans, less than a hundred at this point, met for the first time separately at the Foundery, a dilapidated ironworks near Finsbury Square on what was then the northern edge of London. Wesley had leased it in 1739; he would replace it in the 1780s with the City Road chapel and his personal dwelling-house. From this point on Wesley ruled out any further association with the Moravians. The following set of *Journal* entries come from August 1740 and are typical of the early days of the movement:

Mon. 4 August . . . In the evening many were gathered together at Long Lane on purpose to make a disturbance: having procured a woman to begin, well known in those parts as neither fearing God nor regarding man. The instant she broke out, I turned full upon her and declared the love our Lord had for her soul. We then prayed that He would confirm the word of His grace. She was struck in the heart and shame covered her face. From her I turned to the rest, who melted away like water, and were as men who had no strength. But surely some of them shall find who is 'their rock and their strong salvation'.

Sun. 10 August. – From Gal.vi.3. I earnestly warned all who had tasted the grace of God 1) not to think they were justified before they had a clear assurance that God had forgiven them their sins; bringing in a calm peace, the love of God, and dominion over all sin. 2) Not to think themselves anything after they had this; but to press forward for the prize of their high calling, even a clean heart, throughly renewed after the image of God, to righteousness and true holiness.

Mon. 11 August. – Forty or fifty of those who were seeking salvation desired leave to spend the night together, at the society-room, in prayer and giving thanks. Before ten I left them, and lay down. But I could have no quiet rest, being quite uneasy in my sleep, as I found others were too, that were asleep in other parts of the house. Between two and three in the morning I was waked and desired to come downstairs. I immediately heard such a confused noise as if a number of men were all putting in the sword. It increased when I came into the room and began to pray. One whom I particularly observed to be roaring aloud for pain was one J— W—, who had always, till then, been very sure that none cried out but hypocrites. So had Mrs Sims also. But she too now cried to God with a loud and bitter cry. It was not long before God heard from his holy place. He spake and all our souls were comforted. He bruised Satan under our feet; and sorrow and sighing fled away.

Sat. 16 August. – I called on one who, being at Long Lane on Monday the 4th instant, was exceeding angry at those that pretended to be in fits, particularly at one who dropped down just by her. She was just going to kick her out of the way, when she dropped down herself, and continued in violent agonies for an hour. Being afraid, when she came to herself, that her mother would judge of her as she had done of others, she resolved to hide it from her. But the moment she came into the house she dropped down in as violent an agony as before. I left her weary and heavy-laden, under a deep sense of the just judgement of God.

The published journal form – it was not a question of publishing the unedited text of a day-to-day diary – was first adopted by George Whitefield to create the impression of a moving line of supernatural occurrences. Wesley used it as a means of publicising, defending and uniting the new Wesleyan societies. These accounts contrast with the statements written by the Bristol women in 1742 [see pp. 104–8, 110–23, 126–9] in the sense that the point of view of the successive volumes of the *Journal* was almost always that of John Wesley himself. The text is honest but not innocent; convinced, but edited.

In the early twenty-first century many of the events which Wesley described as evidence of the power of God in human life may seem either unremarkable or eccentric, because similar stories are frequently reported both in print and on television, especially from what are usually called the Protestant 'fundamentalist' reaches of contemporary Christianity. And British broadsheet newspapers regularly carry accounts of alleged Roman Catholic miracles. These stories have little impact on the world outside religious institutions. When, however, in the time of President Ronald Reagan, for example, the leaders of American evangelical Protestanism tried to transform their religious base into a source of direct political influence and even power, the secular culture reacted with hostility. Behind this conflict lay the fact that by the middle of the twentieth century American Protestantism had ceased to dominate the national culture on the religous side, and the emergence of the 'Religious Right' in the 1970s, well equipped with supernatural power, was seen as an attempt to recover the old ascendancy. Crucial to the secular resistance was the reinterpretation of what claimed to be a religious movement concerned with morality, as a movement above all concerned with politics and power. Critics might concede a kind of innocence to primary religion, with its anxious search for security and health, and grant that it expressed an individual need for some kind of supernatural attention, but they did not believe that religious institutions which had entered the political arena were likely to continue to behave innocently.

Between 1740 and the 1760s Anglican critics thought that the expanding Wesleyan societies, sometimes described as Dissenting, occasionally as Roman Catholic, wanted to obtain political influence. The stories which Wesley told in his *Journal* strengthened the feeling that seventeenth-century religious radicalism had revived. This helps to explain the frequent local hostility, which sometimes became violent, when Wesleyanism tried to enter a new village. From time to time a parson or a landowner was to be found encouraging the expulsion of these strangers. The Anglicans thought of themselves as protecting social peace by preventing the planting of new Dissenting churches in the countryside. They easily identified religious enthusiasm – a word which in this context referred to the kind of incidents and attitudes described in the extracts above from Wesley's *Journal* – with a critical attitude to the existing distribution of power in society. Under the Hanoverians Dissent had been reduced to a depressed minority and Roman Catholicism verged on the socially invisible, but both had survived and shaped part of the English consciousness. Wesley himself thought of his success in releasing religious energies as likely to reinforce the existing social system, but in the formative years of the Wesleyan movement he was far from convincing his Anglican critics that this was true.

We may attempt to describe, but we cannot experience, the impact on the Anglican mind of the long struggle with independent Protestantism that seemed to have reached a conclusion in 1714. Imagination cannot really cope with duration, the accumulation of experience decade after decade. The American War of Independence in the 1770s seemed to many Anglicans only to confirm an interpretation of English religion and politics in which the forces of Dissent worked restlessly to overthrow both the Elizabethan and the Hanoverian settlements. In eighteenth-century England Protestantism was the dominant religious form of the national culture, but there was no simple relationship between the various forms of Protestantism and the political regime. This was a divided society, not an organically united one. Neither John nor Charles Wesley could make the Wesleyan societies either socially or religiously part of the established Church, because the majority of people who joined the societies felt that they were rejecting not the established Church as a great religious and political myth but the authority of their local parson and their obligation to accept his views on religion and society. In turn, this did not necessarily mean that they were choosing Dissent, only that they were setting themselves free from some of their apparent obligations – yet this the local Anglican ministry often bitterly resented. They resented it all the more as they realised that some of the Wesleyan itinerants did want to become ministers in their own right.

The Anglican bishops rejected Wesleyanism partly because they sympathised with their parochial clergy and partly because they mistrusted the evidence for a divinely inspired revival of religion which John Wesley was putting forward. A good example of this religious criticism can be found in 1773, when the second generation of Wesleyanism already looked like becoming a permanent institution. In that year

Richard Graves (1715–1804), an Anglican country clergyman but a man by no means out of touch with the sophisticated world, published his novel *The Spiritual Quixote*.

Graves was rector of Claverton, near Bath, from 1749 to his death. He had known George Whitefield, and was a friend of Ralph Allen (1694–1764) of Bath, who combined great wealth with taste and enthusiasm for literature, and of William Shenstone (1714–63), a landscape gardener and minor pastoral poet. When Graves wanted to describe Methodism, a word by this time used indiscriminately for both Wesleyanism and evangelical Anglicanism, he deliberately took images and phrases from the *Journal* entry of 11 August 1740 (see above), combining them with material from George Whitefield's *Journal* for 20 March 1739:

[From Wesley] But, about two in the morning Mr Wildgoose was waked by a confused notion, as if a number of men were putting to the sword. He went up into the Society-room, where the people had worked themselves up to such a pitch of religious phrenzy, that some were fallen prostrate on the floor, screaming, and roaring, and beating their breasts, in agonies of remorse for their former wicked lives; others were singing hymns, leaping and exulting in ecstasies of joy, that their sins were forgiven them. [Now Whitefield] Amongst the rest there was a little boy, of three years old, who had caught the infection, and acted the Sinner with as much appearance of contrition as the best of them. [Now Wesley] The uproar increased when Wildgoose came into the room, and began to pray with them: but Nature, having now been strained to its height for some hours, subsided into a calm. Wildgoose, therefore, dismissed them with a short exhortation.[12]

Graves described his protagonist, Wildgoose, as a squire's son from a village 'under the Cotswold hills'.[13] In a recognisable mood of youthful rebellion against moderate or civil Anglicanism, Wildgoose had read enough Puritan piety to welcome Methodist preaching when he heard it; he became an elegant, sincere and temporary dropout and conducted his own preaching-tour through Bristol, Gloucester, the Forest of Dean, Tewkesbury and the Peak, finally reaching Warwick, where a blow on his head at the racecourse restored him to a sense of his inherited rank and to the Church of England as Graves understood it.

Graves was a representative figure. As a local clergyman he knew at first hand and disliked Wesleyanism, essentially as a possible source of social disintegration. He put the moderate Anglican judgement on itinerant, aggressive evangelicalism into the mouth of Dr Greville, Wildgoose's fictional parson. When Wildgoose said that surely everyone had a divine calling to 'endeavour to revive the practice of true Christianity', Greville replied that they should do so 'by their example and their persuasion, within the sphere of their own neighbourhood', but that no one 'has a right to break through the regulations of society merely from the suggestions of his own fancy, unless he can give some visible proof of a supernatural commission'.[14]

Greville was not inventing this argument, but continuing the line of questioning laid down, for example, in 1744 by Edmund Gibson as bishop of London, when he asked whether 'the strong expressions which are to be found in their Journals of extraordinary presences of God directing and assisting them in a more immediate manner, do not need some Testimonial of a divine mission, to clear them from the charge of Enthusiasm?'[15] The accusation of breaking 'through the regulations of society' meant that the real result of forming Wesleyan societies was seen less as the revival of true Christianity than as the upsetting of the social and religious balance of the local community, releasing discontents and animosities which ought to be kept under control.[16] The argument about 'a supernatural commission' was also important, because seventeenth-century religious radicals had sometimes claimed supernatural authority, and because John Wesley's own accounts of the origins of his movement appealed both to the evidence of dramatic religious activity – there was at least the implication of direct providential intervention, though there was no downright claim to personal possession of miraculous powers – and to the idea that God had specially 'raised up' the Wesleyans to purge the Church and to save the nation.

Although Richard Graves treated Wesley much more mildly than he did George Whitefield, of whom it might be said that he was at his most convincing in the pulpit, it is still true that in the scene quoted above Wildgoose was meant to be playing Wesley's part. Graves did not suggest that Wesley was a mountebank – this was the contemporary satirical view of Whitefield – but that he was a sincere, unironical man, who did not see into the heart of what he was doing and so would always in the end be betrayed by unexpected events. Graves thought that Wesley's judgement was defective: Wesley (he implied) identified the phenomena of primary religion (though obviously Graves would not have used this term) too easily with the essence of Christianity. Graves did not think that one could trust the kind of evidence to which Wesley gave credit. Anglicanism understood, or believed itself to understand, the social nature of Christianity, the relationship between religion and order and obedience. Wesley, in Graves's view, imagined that he agreed with that Tory view of society, but he encouraged the opposite, Dissenting view. This was hardly unfair comment on the Wesley of the 1740s and 1750s.

As Anglican novelists, Richard Graves and Henry Fielding (1707–54), who published *Tom Jones* in 1749, both discussed Anglicanism as a social religion. The same emphasis on the parish as the active theatre of religion can be found in

Samuel Richardson's *Sir Charles Grandison* (1753–54).[17] When Sir Charles, designed by the author as a lay example of the best kind of 'Church of England man', was asked why he did not sometimes preach to the company at his table, he replied that 'it would be an affront to the understanding, as well as education, of a man who took rank above a peasant, in such a country as this, to seem to question whether he knew his general duties or not, and the necessity of practising what he knew of them. If he should be at a loss, he may once a week be reminded, and his heart kept warm.'[18] One should not invade the clergyman's province, and by implication his territorial parish, though it was also one's duty to ensure as far as possible that a suitable clergyman was appointed. And the right man would not only tell the gentry what their responsibilities were to those who lived and worked on their estates, he would also see that their hearts were 'kept warm'. No one who has read the last stages of the tragedy of *Clarissa* – (1747–8) should have any doubt about Richardson's existential grasp of a certain kind of very destructive evangelical piety, but in *Grandison* he is talking about a kind of civil piety, a culture of benevolence, which would draw its warmth from the sayings of the prophets and the teaching of Jesus.

It is not surprising, therefore, that when Richardson mentioned the Methodists with respect, he did so because they had 'given a face of religion to subterranean colliers, tinners, and the most profligate of men, who hardly ever before heard either of the word, or the thing'.[19] He was referring presumably to the miners of Kingswood, near Bristol, and to Cornish tinworkers; his information probably came from Wesley's *Journal*, and he repeated it with approval because in this case he was assuming that in these areas the parochial and landowning system had broken down. This did not mean for him that the system could not cope, or that a religious revival of the Wesleyan kind was needed to put such matters right. Richardson thought that the Anglican bishops, working in agreement with landowners and businessmen who accepted their social and religious responsibilities, and who were willing to support efficient clergymen, were able to ensure that the parish, as the basic social unit, functioned effectively. It was not obvious in the 1750s that the combination of a population explosion with economic expansion was about to wreck the Anglican parish sysem in wide parts of the country. As those changes took place, the grip of the Anglican pattern was weakened steadily. The industrial district of Kingswood, for example, was divided as the century went on by congregations belonging to Anglicans, Moravians, Wesleyans and Whitefieldites.

Moderate Anglicans still thought in terms of the parish as a self-sufficient entity. They looked for a way to reconcile the destructive passions so swiftly evoked by piety with the plain needs of social policy. For them the Establishment was much more than a political convenience, and the relationship between the incumbent and the people of the parish was very different from that between a pastor and his gathered congregation. The Hanoverian Church of England was a national institution, at once religious, political and educational, an arm of the state whose function was to support the Protestant dynasty and to create a civil society. The mass of the population, the desperately poor in the countryside and the marginal inhabitants of larger villages and towns, had to be trained in a pattern of life and belief, especially moral belief, which would help rather than hinder the formation of a peaceful, hierarchical community. Moderate Anglicans did not want the congregation of the parish church to become a Wesleyan society dedicated to the pursuit of religious 'revival'. The social consequences would be unbearable. They valued tolerance more highly than 'revival'.

The Wesleyans, on the other hand, interpreted this Anglican emphasis on the social role of the Establishment as evidence that the clergy were ignorant of the gospel. They moved, against their will, in the direction of Dissent, which rejected the parochial system and was never completely reconciled to the Hanoverian settlement. There was that much truth in the Anglican suspicion of Disssent, but there was no question of the Wesleyans imitating the radicalism which some Dissenting intellectuals showed during the American War of Independence in the 1770s and in the early years of the French Revolution.

To apply words such as 'pelagian' or 'humanist' to the Anglican attitude is to neglect the historical context. The previous two centuries had been filled with passionate Christian division and warfare. Christian missions had carried intolerance deeply into the heart of indigenous cultures in South America and Asia. There had been faith in plenty: the failures of Christian policy and leadership could not be attributed to the sinfulness of individuals, and the religious institutions within which they had lived their lives be thus exonerated. There had been no sign that concentrating on the mysteries of Christianity had solved the problems, either in Protestant or in Roman Catholic countries, of translating religious belief and devotion into tolerant, moral societies. Wesley was addressing a divided English society, whose divisions increased as industrialism expanded and large cities began to form. There was no peaceful organic community united by common beliefs and ethical standards; rather, a society which was growing tired of past slogans and parties.

For many Anglicans religious mystery had for the moment lost its self-justifying power. They preferred a form of Christianity which demanded a socially responsible attitude to money: increased concern for the provision of orphanages, hospitals and poor relief in general, as well as efforts to restore harmony in difficult family and other social relationships. In *The Dissenters* (1978) Michael Watts noted that the great innovators in English religious history – John Smyth, George Fox, the Wesleys – had all placed great emphasis on the work of the Spirit. Watts approved of this tradition, and criticised Joseph Priestley, the late eighteenth-century Socinian intellectual, who stood at the radical margin of Dissent, for combating the notion of Spirit.

Moderate Anglicans, however, were as sceptical of Smyth, Fox and the Wesleys as religious teachers as they were of Priestley. They understood the Hobbesian philosopher Mandeville (1670–1733), for example, when he affected to want purity of motive yet denied that it was possible to achieve it. They distrusted Wesley when he asserted that purity of motive was a divine gift of the Spirit which personal faith might obtain at any moment.

By the early eighteenth century many people wanted a politer, more prosperous, more tolerant and more rationally moral society. They wanted 'improvement', as they often said, not perfection. The attitude to institutional religion was changing: many educated people had come to the conclusion that a Europe socially and morally policed by the professionally religious and the institutions which they directed was no longer a desirable goal. Given political authority, the saint was apt to become like any other political extremist, convinced that his opponents ought not to exist. Montaigne, who had proposed, with reference to witchcraft, that it was putting a very high price on one's conjectures to roast a man alive for them, had for the time being won the argument. His transformation of beliefs into conjectures was deliberate: there was no secure basis for the Churches' claims to invade the political and legal sphere.

To much Roman Catholic and Protestant thought this was intolerable – and the word should carry its full meaning here. To suppose that the increasingly secular state could be the 'saviour' of its people, that the Churches should be confined to what power they could retain over private life, was considered outrageous. The future was made plain in America, where the demand for independence from Britain was not made in specifically Christian language: the independence from a religious establishment of the new United States was part of the American revolution, and nationalism competed with loyalty to the Church as a social binding-force. It was not an accident that by the time the Republican George W. Bush secured the presidency in 2001 the Religious Right was demanding the restoration of the Churches' social hegemony. The same aim, quite as much as any revival of the gospel, lay at the heart of the myth of the eighteenth-century evangelical revival.

Eighteenth-century Anglicanism was freer than Wesleyanism to experiment with cultural changes such as the critical and historical downgrading of the New Testament. The English established Church survived the American rebellion, but in the United States it became one voluntarist church among others. If the tendency of the emerging secular society was to regard religious behaviour as an individual, even private matter, this left Wesleyanism – as a fusion of intellect and emotion in which emotion usually had the upper hand – well placed for the moment to occupy a nonpolitical position, but this did not affect the way in which the Anglican episcopate regarded the Wesleyan societies. In the first decade of the nineteenth century Anglican politicians, shaken by their experiences of the previous forty years, still instinctively wanted to stop Wesleyan growth.

The nature of the official Anglican reaction to the general phenomenon of Methodism can be examined in some hostile notes which Archbishop Secker made on letters which the Reverend John Berridge (1716–93), an evangelical Anglican of the second generation of Wesleyanism, wrote in 1758 to a neighbouring vicar, Dr Poynton, who in turn passed them on to Secker for comment. Berridge had become a prominent itinerant in the Midlands from a base near Cambridge and was for some years on friendly terms with the Wesleys. The experiences which Berridge described, together with Secker's rejection of them, have to be included here, because they represent two sides of the Anglican response to Wesleyanism. Anglicanism, after all, is relatively easy to define at the institutional level, as the Church of the state and possibly of the nation. It was established by law in the sixteenth century, and its legal rights and duties have been modified from time to time ever since, without the idea of an official Church being formally renounced. The Church of England could be said to exist to save the English from Rome: it did not have to be the Church of the majority to play that role. The agreed intellectual content of the word Anglicanism was as much political as theological. No one secondary theological system achieved permanent control at the official level.

Berridge, who began local itinerancy as an evangelical in the 1750s, entered what was already becoming a tradition of semi-Dissent. He was one of a group of individualistic clergymen who were fascinated by the claims which men like Whitefield and the Wesleys were making about the results of faith, and were prepared to imitate them. Some of them associated with the Countess of Huntingdon, who offered them social protection. An example of a quite different, but equally rural, clergyman would be James Woodforde (1740–1803), rector of Weston Longeville in Norfolk from 1774 until his death, whose faithful description of enormous meals, often provided by his local squire, has so delighted many modern readers of his diary that they overlook a deep strain of civic piety.[20]

A Cambridge graduate, born in 1716, Berridge had in 1755 become incumbent of Everton, a very small parish which lay between Bedford and Cambridge, and he stayed there until he died. Soon after his arrival in Everton Berridge had a personal crisis, which he described in a letter dated 3 July 1758. He had for years, he wrote, preached that people were to be justified partly by their faith and partly by their works. He grew uneasy, however, because his preaching did not seem to him to affect the lives of his hearers. This is a common but destructive experience for the conscientious priest, and happens when he admits to himself for the first time that his hearers have their own patterns of religious and secular behaviour, which are not deeply affected by what he says or does. Berridge prayed earnestly for guidance (effectively, for the power to affect his parishioners), and, as he put it, the following words were darted into his mind with wonderful power, and seemed like a voice from heaven: 'Cease from thy works.' The implication, as Secker read it, was not that Berridge had remembered a passage which he thought came from the Bible and which seemed to him to suggest a solution, but that he thought the Spirit had intervened to advise him. This way of putting it was common among Wesleyan itinerants at the time.

Secker did not regard these words as relevant. 'These are not the words of Scripture,' he wrote. 'The Jews are blamed Judges 2.19 for not ceasing from their own wicked doings, and Solomon saith labour not to be rich, cease from thine own wisdom Proverbs 23.4. But these texts are not to his purpose, so his opinion was changed neither by Reason nor Scripture, but by a seeming voice from Heaven.'[21] Secker was placing what had happened to Berridge outside the religious sphere: Berridge had changed his opinion, but was not entitled to claim divine authority for doing so.

Berridge, foreseeing this kind of reaction, had noted that before he heard these words he was unusually calm, but that after them he was immediately in a tempest: tears flowed like a torrent and the scales fell from his eyes:

When a man is convinced of sin, he feels what he never knew before, that he hath no Faith, and in this state men continue a longer or a shorter time, till God works faith in them, and then they know that they are forgiven. After that sanctification goes onward, and they are filled with Joy and Peace.

Secker added another note:

By faith he means a full persuasion that God through Christ hath forgiven him. Whether this be justifying faith, see more clearly afterwards. Only observe here, that men, convinced they have sinned, may be falsely persuaded, that God has forgiven them, for so he supposes himself to have been for many years.

Secker's caution as regards subjective Christian experience, and claims to have received direct spiritual guidance, have to be set in a secondary theological context. During the Reformation the question of whether contemporary – that is, sixteenth-century – supernatural activity, in the form of visions, acts of healing and direct inspiration by the Spirit, was still taking place, had become a fundamental issue. Roman Catholic apologists defended the opinion that events of this kind were evidentiary marks of the true ecclesia, and claimed that the Roman Church possessed these marks, whereas (they said) the Protestant Churches did not. Catholic writers had the advantage that this particular speculative theological notion appealed, as one would expect, to primary religious impulses, so much so that the European recovery of Catholicism in the seventeenth century was deeply indebted to a policy of concentrating the appeal of the supernatural (and its availability) on Marian sites throughout mainland Europe. Protestant theologians developed the equally speculative theory that the Roman Church had fallen under the power of Antichrist, and concluded that in the corrupt state of the Church there could be no reliance on any apparently supernatural intervention because such events might be deceptive activity on the part of the instruments of darkness.

The theological arguments were accompanied by Protestant action, going far beyond the occasional outbreaks of iconoclasm, which have attracted more attention than they merit. The reformed Church of England, supported by the state, not only rejected the view that miraculous powers had continued in the Church down to the present, but swept away the whole visible Catholic apparatus of supernatural assistance: local shrines and pilgrimage centres, with all their furniture of statues, pictures, relics and ex-votos, the theatre in which primary religion and theology had overlapped and interacted for centuries, disappeared. The intellectual climate, in which the prevailing influences had come from classical and scriptural sources, also altered, not because these sources were abandoned, but because their authority was more deeply questioned than ever before, and because new sources of information began to accumulate. There was, as one American scholar has recently observed:

a shift in Christian experience and affirmation asserted by the Protestant denial of contemporary miracle and its hagiological context. Within a generation or two, the actual pneumatic visage of the Church was wholly redescribed, and in a way that can only be admitted as being utterly novel.[22]

In England the religious landscape changed. By the time Wesleyanism took shape as a network of interconnected societies, painting and sculpture, which had filled the primary religious imagination with familiar figures, naturalising the supernatural, had ceased to play a significant part in English Protestant experience. Protestantism filled the imaginative space that remained in its own way, as when the early Wesleyans had vivid visions of both the Father and the Son; but no secondary theology developed remotely like the seventeenth-century European Catholic devotion to the Sacred Heart of Jesus, for instance, a cult of reparative suffering associated with John Eudes and Marguerite-Marie Alacoque,[23] which has survived into modern Vatican devotional theology. One of the central obsessions of Alacoque's visions was the need to drive Protestantism out of seventeenth-century France, and she bears some responsibility for the persecution and exile of the Huguenots. Politics took precedence over piety and pity. Although Secker's response to Berridge's interest in Wesleyanism did not take the form of a direct suggestion that the evangelicals and Wesleyans were readopting Roman Catholic positions, his views derived from the anxiety of Church of England theologians to draw a thick line between themselves and Continental Catholicism.

Later Anglo-Catholic and Roman Catholic attempts to write the Reformation out of English history, except as an unfortunate lapse of taste which can now be ignored, have distorted our perception of what happened. A largely inexplicable change in cultural attitude took place, which was not as isolated or disastrous as is sometimes suggested. The disappearance of art from most English churches was the equivalent of the equally sudden proliferation of naked gods and goddesses in European painting: Christian images and metaphors had begun to lose their religious power, as Mars and Venus edged out the Virgin and Child. The long reign of the inspirational romantic landscape began. The local English parish church may have lost some of its aura as a centre of the cult of a saint, but the eucharist continued to be celebrated. Roman Catholic writers have always exaggerated the effect of the change from the mass to the holy communion, because they failed to distinguish adequately between the concepts of religion and Christianity, and supposed that their own devotional theology exhausted the possible experiential, and indeed the Christian, content of such rites. There was no 'stripping' of the altars, no contrast between devotional emptiness (Protestant) and a convincing sacrifice of the mass (Roman Catholic). By the time that Secker was writing his notes on Berridge's letters, many Anglicans had hardened their attitude towards those who believed that they could bring supernatural power directly into the community, either through the invocation of Mary and the saints, or through the invocation of the Holy Spirit.

Secker's attitude to Berridge was not therefore evidence of a decline of Christianity on his side, and the rediscovery of Christian truth on the other. He objected to Berridge's statement that watching, praying and fasting could not purify men's hearts, but that faith could do this, and he commented: 'he will surely own, that after previous faith there are means, without which previous faith will purifie and sanctifie us very insufficiently, if at all'.[24] This was the crucial distinction as far as Secker was concerned. He thought that self-conscious moral analysis determined the quality of the human response to what was known of the will of God. He did not expect that the quality of human judgement would be very high, but he did not think that faith would sanctify by itself, and so he was equally opposed to Wesleyanism as to Berridge.

Secker was just as unimpressed by Berridge's assertion that his personal sinfulness had been preventing the Holy Spirit from working through him to convert those who heard him preach. Nor did he agree that holiness, if it came at all, came

by faith alone. Berridge thought that the Spirit had deliv-
ered him from the bondage of the self: Secker, rationally (and
sensibly) cautious about anyone's ability to identify the Spirit's
activity, thought that Berridge was the victim of linguistic self-
deception. Berridge asserted that his new preaching, 'that
by any one sin, they were lost without Christ', brought him
hearers from six to ten miles around. He went on, in a style not
unfamiliar in the revivalist world, to make a strong attack on
human learning and divinity, and declared 'that every believer
is taught by the Spirit all needful truth, and therefore is qualified to preach, if he hath the gift of utterance'. Secker noted:
'is this a qualification sufficient, unless a man can also prove
them by proper evidence and distinguish them from Hay and
Stubble?'[25] The objection was just as relevant to some of the
Wesleyan preachers.

In the final part of his letter Berridge came to the point
which he felt proved his case, talking about the consequences
of his changed style of preaching:

> If they, who are thought religious, are asked, whether they know they
> are forgiven, and feel joy in the Holy Ghost, they will think you an
> Enthusiast. Now these are only almost Christians . . . and such as feel
> their need of Christ find not proper food for their souls in our Church,
> and are forced to seek it where they can . . . for the last century, almost
> all the clergy have preached justification partly by works.

Berridge granted that the Church of England had during the sixteenth-century Reformation returned to the true
faith in Christ, 'but our own clergy departed once more from
him. About twenty years since God raised up Mr Whitefield,
Mr Wesley and others.' Secker did not accept this picture
of a general apostasy of the clergy which God had intervened to set right. Berridge, however, was committed to the
idea of a divinely inspired revival, and said that at Christmas

he had been told that forty clergymen were brought to the acknowledgement of the truth, and three more within the past eight weeks.[26]

Historians have to accept Berridge's statement that what he and many others believed was, as he told his hearers in Cambridgeshire, 'that by any one sin, they were lost without Christ'. They do not, though, have to regard this as a profound truth about either God or humanity, and may sympathise with Secker's reaction when Dr Poynton, who had replied to Berridge's original letter on 20 November 1758, passed on a second letter from Berridge which he had received on 28 November. Here Berridge stated, for example, that 'advising a sinner to repent and do better, is sending him to that Law to save him, which must condemn him. Law, of God or man, as Law, can show no mercy.' He asserted that 'where the Law is revealed it binds; and when broken, denounces a curse, and nothing can remove it but faith', and faith was communicated by God's Spirit to those who, 'having felt their lost estate, seek earnestly after it'.[27] 'Faith', he declared, 'is not in the Head, but in the Heart.'[28] Above all, faith was not believing doctrines about Christ, but was 'such a reliance on Christ, wrought on us by the Spirit, as assures our hearts that God is reconciled to us . . . knowing that Christ loveth me and hath died for me Gal 2.20'.

One can see the attractiveness of all this. Berridge himself desperately needed to feel that he was not a failure, that the deity was on his side and that he was not already condemned to an eternity of suffering and remorse. He wanted to feel at home in a benevolent universe, at least as far as he and his local community were concerned. For years the destructive side of the Christian worldview had nagged at his consciousness: now it seemed that his consciousness could be filled with a sense of divine approval.

Secker disagreed with everything Berridge said. He argued that the 'laws of man can punish crimes less than they deserve, or can provide for relaxation of punishment in certain circumstances, or even for impunities'. Similarly, God was not bound by the letter of his own law. As for faith, 'strictly speaking', Secker wrote, '[it] is neither in the Head nor in the Heart, but in the Mind. But heart in Scripture sometimes means the Mind, and even the intellectual part of it.' He rejected Berridge's description of faith – there were various ways of describing faith in Scripture, 'but this is never the description of it there, and therefore it is not the true one, and believing oneself to be pardoned is as much a speculative faith as believing all penitents to be pardoned'.[29] And 'are not this feeling and this seeking', the Archbishop enquired at a later point, 'works of the mind, and may it not be said . . . that this is being justified partly by Works and partly by Faith?'[30]

Secker was contradicting the black-and-white attitude which was at the root of Berridge's system, as it was of Wesley's and Whitefield's. Secker thought that the evangelical position was ethically deficient, and he distrusted Berridge's appeal to what we might call an altered state of consciousness, which was supposed to be the result of divine intervention. As Secker saw it, the evangelicals had little sympathy with the domestic problems and sufferings of the individuals who made up their congregations, people who were often poorly educated, sexually and socially driven, in need of money. For the new school of preachers the words 'fallen' and 'saved' were becoming a complete psychology. 'Fallen' was used as a theological abstraction, a term of art which pointed to a wretched creature who was already judged and condemned by God, who might – or in the more extreme Calvinist cases might not – offer faith as the only way out. Anglicans such as Secker were arguing for a reasonable, mixed spirituality, in which one did what one could in terms of faith and works, and trusted God for the outcome. Berridge, on the other hand, had totally committed himself against works, and closed his letter with a denunciation of the Epistle of James – he naturally could not accept James's assertion that 'faith without works is dead'. What was dead was works without faith as he defined it.

The Archbishop counterattacked sharply:

can then anyone know, that he hath saving faith, but by its producing works? And if not, can any other Feelings ascertain our state? Hereby we know, that we know Him, i.e. believe on Him right, if we keep his commandments. James opposes a notional belief, not to a belief that Christ has procured pardon of my sins, which is just as notional, but to Works [produced] by Faith, or Faith producing Works, between which he seems not to think it worth distinguishing.[31]

It is not clear that Secker understood the risks he was running when he insisted that the proper test of meaningful religious belief was behaviour. He did not think of English Protestantism as one of many possible patterns of thought which might enable a community to claim divine authority for its ethical system. But he was well aware that a functioning society needed a set of broad rules which most people kept most of the time, and that the established Church was widely valued as a national teacher of such rules. In Secker's opinion the Church of England could not afford to direct too much of its energy into the pursuit of Wesleyan states of consciousness for which much might be claimed in popular preaching and devotional treatises, but which seemed to have divisive social consequences. Moderate Anglicans did not accept a description of Christianity which relied on personal faith to generate an ethically renewed personality. And to introduce ideas of perfection into the world of primary religion (although this vocabulary would not have been used in the eighteenth century) was to invite disaster. When some Wesleyans claimed that they had not, for some time past, consciously sinned – and this claim could certainly be heard in London in the early 1760s – the Anglican hierarchy were unlikely to approve what they heard.

Another version of the episcopal position in the mid-eighteenth century was put, rather brutally, by William Warburton, (1698–1779), bishop of Gloucester, who had a reputation as a controversialist. He published *The Doctrine of Grace; or the Offices and Operations of the Holy Spirit vindicated from the insults of Infidelity and the abuses of Fanaticism* in 1763. Warburton's choice of passages from Wesley's *Journals* was dismissed by Gordon Rupp, with the comment: 'Once again an opponent was able to exploit the scores of case histories, of which Wesley made so much, and which were so interlarded with Scriptural allusions and particular and providential answers to prayer, as to distract attention from the real heart of the revival, to which they were by no means essential, and even, in the long run, irrelevant.'[32] This was not, in my view, how the passages would have been read in the eighteenth century, and I doubt whether, in the twenty-first century, such passages in the *Journals* should be treated as either inessential or irrelevant to the heart of the movement. As far as the period from the 1730s to the 1760s was concerned, they were at the heart of Wesleyanism's success, and contemporaries knew it.

Here one example will suffice. Warburton had picked out of an early *Journal* (in the entry for 20 December 1742) the statement: 'Mr Meyrick had been speechless and senseless for some time. A few of us joined in prayer. Before we had done his sense and speech returned. Others may account for this by natural causes. I believe this is the power of God.' Wesley now (in 1763, twenty years later) replied to Warburton:

But what does all this prove? Not that I claim any gift above other men, but only that I believe that God now hears and answers prayer, even beyond the ordinary course of nature. Otherwise the clerk was in the right who (in order to prevent the fanaticism of his rector) told him, 'Sir, you should not pray for fair weather yet, for the moon does not change till Saturday.'[33]

Warburton had gone too far in attacking Wesley on the ground that he had claimed to have miraculous powers, and Wesley was able to sidestep the blow, but Wesley also reaffirmed his earlier belief that Meyrick had been brought round by prayer, and Warburton's moderate Anglican readers were hardly likely to miss the point of the statement that God answered prayer 'even beyond the ordinary course of nature'. Wesley used the anecdote about the scepticism of the clerk to point out that the Church of England prayed for favourable weather, but by the 1760s the clerk was not the only person doubtful about that.

Wesley's accounts of dramatic events of this kind, including the quite specific (and primary) example of a successful collective quest for healing, lay at the heart of his theological position, because they constituted his evidence that the Holy Spirit which was said to have acted in the New Testament period was also present in the eighteenth century, and could be encountered not only in one's heart but also in the external world, as in cases of healing like that of Mr Meyrick. In replying to Warburton, Wesley quoted arguments he had already employed in 1749, when he tried to answer Conyers Middleton (1683–1750), a liberal Anglican who had used historical criticism to ridicule the miracle stories told by the Church Fathers, and had implied that the miracle narratives of the New Testament had no stronger foundations.[34]

Warburton, Middleton and Wesley illustrate the range of opinion to be found in eighteenth-century Anglicanism. Warburton stood for the soft centre, that is, for the view that there was no need to look too deeply into orthodox Protestantism, and that although miraculous powers had existed for

some time in the post-New Testament Church, they had certainly been withdrawn altogether by the Dark Ages. Leslie
Stephen's description of Warburton's reaction to Wesley was
certainly overdone: 'when poor Wesley was rash enough to
publish those accounts of modern miracles with which his
journals are so curiously stuffed, the episcopal wrath knew
no bounds. That a man living in his own time, and that man
an ecclesiastical rebel, should produce miracles to confirm his
foolish fancies was intolerable.'[35]

'Poor Wesley' could look after himself in controversy, in
which he invariably regarded himself as victorious, and the
phrase 'curiously stuffed' betrays the case which Stephen was
making. Stephen sneered at Warburton for taking what was
Stephen's own view – that there were no 'modern miracles' –
because he found it intolerable that a bishop should take the
correct position.

Conyers Middleton was more deeply disturbed about
the religious situation than either Warburton or Wesley.
He belonged to a late seventeenth and early eighteenth-
century group of intellectuals for whom the emotional link
to Christianity had been broken. Middleton represented the
critical future. He recognised that Christianity was theologically overloaded; he doubted that miraculous interventions of
the kind which tradition described had ever happened; he had
more in common with Hume and Gibbon than with the apologists for orthodoxy. The forms which primary religion was
taking in movements such as Wesleyanism did not touch him,
so that, like Warburton, he found Wesley either irrelevant or
irritating.

Wesley repeated in 1763 what he had said in 1749 to
Middleton, that if one had Christian faith as Wesley defined
it and the Wesleyans knew it, one had a radical subjective
certainty of the truth of Christianity, because faith 'gives a

more extensive knowledge of things invisible, showing what eye had not seen, nor ear heard, neither could it enter into our heart to conceive. And all these it shows in the clearest light, with the fullest certainty and evidence.'[36] The traditional evidences of the truth of Christianity, derived from the alleged fulfilment of Old Testament prophecies in the life of Jesus, and from the supernatural powers displayed in the history of the Primitive Church, were all very well, Wesley conceded, and he did not reject them, or suppose that they could be disproved, but:

I have sometimes been almost inclined to believe that the wisdom of God has, in latter ages, permitted the external evidence of Christianity to be more or less clogged and encumbered for this very end, that men (of reflection especially) might not altogether rest there, but be constrained to look into themselves also, and attend to the light shining in their hearts.[37]

This anti-intellectual argument, which became popular again in late twentieth-century theology, was useful against Middleton, because it enabled Wesley to move the grounds for belief from the historic past to the present and from tradition to the individual consciousness, and imply that Middleton was trusting his head when he should be trusting his heart. It was less effective against Warburton's position because Warburton had already cast doubt on the individual's ability to grasp correctly what was happening to him religiously. Special providences and experiential religion (Wesley's phrase) were just as much matters of opinion, according to Warburton, as patristic miracle stories, which the bishop as a good Anglican was not obliged to believe, even when they were reported by someone like Augustine. Put more indirectly, and more subtly, this was Richard Graves's approach in *The Spiritual Quixote* (see pp. 150–3). Both the Anglican novelist and the bishop thought that the new religious movements were overdependent on theological explanations of what people felt that they felt; both doubted that one could distinguish between Roman Catholic and Wesleyan claims about divine activity.

In his reply to Warburton (and Middleton) Wesley wrote:

traditional evidence [as defined above] is of an extremely complicated nature, necessarily including so many and so various considerations that only men of strong and clear understanding can be sensible of its full force. On the contrary, how plain and simple is this [that is, the appeal to 'internal evidence']. And how level to the lowest capacity. Is this not the sum? 'One thing I know: I was blind, but now I see' [John 9: 25]. An argument so plain that a peasant, a woman, a child may feel its force.

It is hardly surprising that some Anglican writers in the 1760s thought that Wesley was not only giving a radically unacceptable description of how the supernatural acted in the human consciousness, but was also defending the possibility of contemporary miracle as the word itself was normally used – 'loosely speaking', as he himself put it. He widened the argument drastically by describing as undeniable the occurrence of 'diabolical miracles, wrought by the power of evil spirits'.[38] This assertion was in line with his lingering, and by the 1760s very old-fashioned, belief in the possibility of witchcraft. In this context – the context of primary religion – his use of a New Testament healing miracle as the climax of the passage quoted above was unlikely to conciliate his critics. He may have intended to say no more than that peasants, women and children – by which he meant groups of uneducated people – could have so strong a sense of having been forgiven, that they *felt* as though they had been 'blind' but were suddenly able to 'see'. The analogy was fair enough, but the process he was trying to describe sounded irrational in a way familiar and disturbing to the moderate Anglican mind.

Wesley committed himself as far as saying that he did not recollect that miracles were to be confined within the limits of either the apostolic or the Cyprianic age, or any period of time, even till the restitution of all things. He went further, arguing that if it were reported that while a clergyman (he meant himself) was preaching, a man came in who had long been ill of an incurable disease, that prayer was made for him and that he was restored to perfect health, then Warburton and his supporters would say that there had been no miracle, that this was just the kind of story that the Wesleyans would tell, that the explanation of what happened was to be found in natural causes, or, at a pinch, that the devil was responsible. The difficulty with this argument was that it left Warburton free to reply that Wesley was claiming that Wesleyan prayer could work miracles. And this claim was not irrelevant to the nature of Wesleyanism, but fundamental to it.

Wesley himself, who was no more a social revolutionary than most Anglicans in the 1760s, tried to be conciliatory, substituting moral for physical transformation. He told Warburton that the real miracle of Wesleyanism was that it was bringing multitudes of gross, notorious sinners, in a short space, to the fear and love and service of God, to an entire change of heart and life. Whereas Warburton criticised Wesleyanism as socially destructive, on the ground that the societies divided local communities, Wesley countered that those who had been renewed would offer what he called 'social love' to the community in which they lived; he avoided any suggestion that the redemption of the social system through personal salvation would have political consequences. There was no question of Wesleyanism reviving George Fox's splendid eschatological contempt for a hierarchical social order. Behind the innocent exterior of Wesley's language lay the image of Wesleyanism as a holiness movement, a valid view in the 1760s, and this in turn suggested the picture of a purified ecclesia reminiscent of the stranger seventeenth-century sects. Moderate Anglicans concluded that Wesley had not altogether lost hope of a dramatic, even eschatological, transformation of society in the near future.

Such impressions could only be strengthened when, again in his answer to Warburton, Wesley seemed to challenge the claim of the Church of England to be a Church at all:

Many of those who were once baptised, and are called Christians to this day, hear the word of God, attend public prayers, and partake of the Lord's Supper. But neither does this prove that they are Christians. For notwithstanding this, some of them live in open sin; and others (though not conscious to themselves of hypocrisy) are utter strangers to the religion of the heart; are full of pride, vanity, covetousness, ambition; of hatred, anger, malice or envy; and consequently, are no more spiritual Christians than the open drunkard or common swearer . . . Now these being removed, where are the Christians? . . . The men who have the mind which was in Christ, and who walk as he walked, whose inmost soul is renewed after the image of God, and who are outwardly holy, as he who hath called them is holy? There are doubtless a few such to be found. To deny this would be a want of candour. But how few? How thinly scattered up and down? And as for a Christian visible church, or a body of Christians visibly united together, where is this to be seen?[39]

The rhetorical device – pitting one ideal type against another to the writer's satisfaction – was not difficult, and similar judgements about the state of the nation were a standard part of the eighteenth-century preacher's armoury. But the question where a body of genuine Christians (as Wesley defined them) can be seen 'visibly united together' could only be treated as rhetorical if one allowed that there never had been such a Church, except possibly the Church of the apostles, and never would be. Otherwise, some of Wesley's Anglican readers were bound to feel that the attack was meant for them, and that it was uncharitable and unjustifiable, not least from an Anglican parson.

Wesley had originally attracted attention as a field-preacher on the edge of eccentricity. At that stage one could quietly disagree with him about the likelihood of witchcraft or ecstatic states of the religious consciousness. It was a different matter when Wesley implied that the established Church was barely a Church at all, and that there was no point in calling England a Christian country. A modern reader might feel that Wesley did not mean to be taken too seriously, that this was the extravagance of an exalted preacher, but by the 1760s Wesleyanism had become well known, and had passed the stage at which Methodists were regarded as an interesting subject for polite conversation.

What we are concerned with here is the variety and nature of Anglican responses. It is interesting, therefore, to place Wesley's broadbrush indictment, and the moderate Anglican rejection of it, in the context of the diary of a very ordinary Anglican layman, Thomas Turner (1729–93).[40] This diary spans the years 1754–65 and therefore is of the same period as the Warburton-Wesley exchange.

In the Sussex village of East Hoathly, not far from Lewes, Turner had a shop but was also a churchwarden, an intelligent and efficient overseer of the poor, a tax-gatherer and an undertaker. He could teach, and he read historical and religious books voraciously, as well as part, at least, of *Clarissa*. At first sight his record of village life might seem to support Wesley's contemptuous question: 'What use is it of, what good end does it serve, to term England "a Christian country"?' Turner himself could exclaim in that style, as for example in 1757: 'dissoluteness of manners, a spirit of effeminacy and self-interest, together with an intolerable share of pride and luxury, seem almost to overspread the whole face of this kingdom'.[41]

East Hoathly itself, a small but not isolated community whose
energies seem to have been largely absorbed in matters of
money, drinking and sex, would probably have struck Wesley
as confirming his judgement. Turner represented the rector,
the Reverend Thomas Porter (1720–94), as a boisterous social drinker and a steady advancer of his family's fortunes;
by Wesley's standards a destructive man, who knew nothing
about scriptural Christianity.

Turner had his own reservations about Porter's behaviour,
but on 17 June 1761, when Turner's first wife was dying, he
recorded that Porter came to his house and 'administered the
communion to my wife and self and servants, and as this in
all human probability will be the last time that we shall ever
commemorate (together in this world) the death of our blessed
Saviour and Redeemer Jesus Christ, so may the memory of it
be a motive to spur me on through God's grace to prepare for
eternity (that awful thought be the first in my mind)'.[42] I do not
suggest that this is an example of the spirit of primary religion.
Turner and his wife asked for comfort at the moment when
death was imminent, and the Church of England responded.
Porter brought them comfort through an objective ceremony
whose efficacy did not depend on Porter's faith or holiness.

The diary, which was not written to make a case for the
village's religious condition, or with any idea of publication, provides a moderate rebuttal of Wesley's analysis of
'Christian England', which depended upon making a distinction between the spiritual, who had been saved, and the remainder of the population, who were 'utterly without Christ
and without God in the world'. Wesley quoted Ephesians 2: 12
to add apostolical authority to his judgement. The distinctions
which one might make between people in this village – distinctions whose value is limited by the horizons of the diarist, as
well as by one's personal moral preferences – do not confirm

Wesley's claim that the majority were utterly without either Christ or God. The most obvious distinction in Hoathly was that between the wealthy and the economically self-sufficient on the one hand, and the poor and the poverty-stricken on the other, and it becomes clear that for all their vanity, hard drinking and financial greed, people with money and power in the village were not totally unaware of a moral and social responsibility, which some of them worked as hard to fulfil as others worked strenuously to avoid. There is no suggestion in the diary that a current of religious revival was influencing the principal people in the place; there is a passing reference to three servants who went to hear a neighbouring Anglican curate who had turned field-preacher in 1763, but what Turner's record reveals is the capacity of the parish to respond to moral concern and unhappiness of conscience.

If Wesleyanism had penetrated Hoathly, Porter and others would certainly have reacted with hostility and perhaps with violence, and some Anglicans would have felt this response was not an entirely mischievous reaction to unnecessary provocation. On the other hand, those who wanted the comforts of primary religion might well have turned towards the invaders in the beginning, as can be seen, perhaps, in the incident of the three servants who went to hear preaching which might have proved exciting.

There was some loss of Anglican confidence, but there is little evidence that the Church of England was provoked into change by the emergence of Whitefield and the Wesleys. There were not enough Wesleyans in either the country towns or the villages by the 1760s to impose a change of consciousness. Evangelical Anglicanism was a choice of individuals, most of whom retained faith in Anglicanism as it was, from established status to parochial machinery. There was a deep unwillingness to interfere with the parish system in any drastic sense.

The new mechanism which transformed eighteenth-century evangelical Anglicanism into one of the three major divisions of the Church of England was not Wesleyan. The Church of England developed not through the parish system but (as was noted in Chapter 3) through the device of the single-issue society, a political device of great flexibility. The evangelical Church Missionary Society, started in 1799, was run on a national basis by a central London Committee with local affiliates, a device natural to the network of wealthy evangelical businessmen, and grew out of the choice, made by William Wilberforce and others in the later years of the century, to make the abolition of the slave trade and of slavery itself a major aim of the national movement. From the point of view of the poor in such places as Wiltshire, the choice of the slave trade as a target was deeply ironic, and in the 1790s, spurred on partly by fear of rural disorder and partly by anxiety about Wesleyan rural expansion, Hannah More and William Wilberforce would turn to the problems of deprivation and poverty as they encountered them in Somerset, where there was a similar dearth of schools in the countryside. They had no effective remedy for the economic problems which were largely responsible for the situation, but more and more Anglican parishes were given schools of a simple sort in the half-century which followed. Wesleyanism moved more slowly, reaching a decision to organise day schools in the late 1830s.

Overseas, Wesleyanism also followed the Anglican example and started its own official national Missionary Society as late as 1818, when Thomas Coke (who was to die on the voyage) set out with a party of six missionaries for Ceylon. There was a kind of evangelical innocence about this choice of destination. The Portuguese had, savagely but successfully, established Roman Catholicism there as far back as the sixteenth century; the Dutch, who replaced them in the seventeenth century but could not establish Calvinism, had been equally intolerant of Buddhism, the religion of the vast majority of the population. When Britain acquired the island at the close of the eighteenth century, it seemed natural to the Wesleyans, who proved vigorous supporters of British imperialism, to make another Protestant assault on Buddhism. In fact, both Buddhism and Hinduism revived during the nineteenth century. At the end of the twentieth century there were about 30,000 Methodists in Ceylon. Sinhalese historians agree that the missionary threat to the traditional culture became the principal cause of modern nationalism in Ceylon. Roman Catholicism remained the dominant Christian community.

Anglicanism also responded to the changing nature of British nationalism, which was entering a more aggressive and Protestant phase. The landed classes (it might be argued), in alliance with a new generation of businessmen with their eyes on the West Indies and the Far East, wanted to make their profitable social hegemony secure, and supported the drive for an overseas empire from the Seven Years War onwards. They welcomed and fostered an accommodating Church, whose clergy were willing to advocate the value of social unity in return for guarantees of their own future in a changing society.

Eighteenth-century Anglican bishops were simply unattracted by what they knew of the Methodists. At the religious level, for example, Archbishop Secker, as we have seen, had genuine doubts about the value of Berridge's religious experience and the claims that he made for it. He interpreted Berridge as a man who deceived himself and lived on religious sensation. Wesley, on the other hand, printed with approval in his *Journal* the composite account of the revival meetings which took place in Everton in 1759. This description emphasised the

presence of 'the power of God', which was confirmed, for instance, by the spectacle of an eight-year-old boy, 'who roared
above his fellows, and seemed, in his agony, to struggle with
the strength of a grown man. His face was as red as scarlet,
and almost all on whom God laid his hand turned either very
red or almost black.'[43] There was also the case of the woman
who had come thirteen miles, and 'is the same person who
dreamed that Mr Berridge would come to her village on that
very day when he did come, though without knowing either
the place or the way to it'.

When Berridge preached on the common at Shelford to,
as he wrote, ten thousand people including 'gownsmen', he
tried to think of 'something pretty to set off with', but could
not, 'so that I broke out with the first word that occurred, not
knowing whether I should be able to add any more; then the
Lord opened my mouth, enabling me to speak near an hour
without any kind of perplexity, and so loud that everyone
might hear'.[44] Equally characteristic was the story:

> there were three farmers, in three several villages, who violently set
> themselves to oppose it [the revival], and for a time they kept many
> from going to hear; but all three died in about a month. One of
> them owned that the hand of the Lord was upon him, and besought
> Him, in the bitterness of his soul, to prolong his life, vowing to hear
> Mr Berridge himself, but the Lord would not be entreated.[45]

Power, which fixes on children as well as on adults, and
which disposes of three critical farmers in a month, including
one who was allegedly anxious to change sides; unprepared
speaking, with the Lord invoked to guarantee the results;
a woman whose dream foretells a visit: this narrative does
not come from a hostile episcopal account, but is an example
of how mid eighteenth-century popular Anglicanism, strug-
gling with its primary religious impulses, described itself in

evangelical language. These were the stories and the experiences which people really wanted from Anglican religious sources: miraculous transformations of the world as it is. They accepted a theology, whether Wesleyan or evangelical Anglican, as part of the bargain, but they were not deeply concerned about it; they already had their own system of belief, which justified the search for a supernatural power. The narrators communicate their pleasure in being part of a wide movement of feeling which isolated those who normally controlled these rural communities, and left them in helpless opposition.

All these were Anglican attitudes with which the bishops had little sympathy. Wesley himself, on the other hand, essentially accepted what the Everton narrator (John Walsh, a converted deist) related. His *Journal* shows that in July 1759, when he was in York, he had begun reading to the Wesleyan society there:

an account of the late work of God at Everton; but I could not get through. At first there were only silent tears on every side, but it was not long before several were unable to refrain from weeping aloud; and quickly a stout young man dropped down and roared as in the agonies of death . . . I did not attempt to read any further, but began wrestling with God in prayer.[46]

Wesley made it clear in a later passage of the *Journal* that he himself expected what he called 'outward symptoms' at the beginning of a general work of God,[47] and he advised those who were in charge to be quite passive, leaving the outcome to God. He gives the impression that by printing these accounts he was trying to teach his followers what to expect and how they ought to react. And, again in the *Journal*, under the date 29 July 1759, he supplied further information about what was going on in Cambridgeshire. Visions and roaring prostrations abound in this second passage. There was also an incident in which the narrator (John Walsh again) found that when he prayed some people:

burst into a strange, involuntary laughter, so that my voice could scarce be heard, and when I strove to speak louder a sudden hoarseness seized me. Then the laughter increased. I perceived it was Satan, and resolved to pray on. Immediately the Lord rebuked him that laughter was at an end . . . a girl about eleven years old, who had been counted one of the wickedest in Harlston, was exceedingly blessed.[48]

It was hardly surprising that official Anglican opinion still remained unenthusiastic in 1759. Wesley's second report on Berridge's meetings suggested that two prominent evangelical Anglicans, Martin Madan (1720–90), who owed his conversion to Whitefield and who had itinerated for the Countess of Huntingdon since 1757, and William Romaine (1714–90), who had favoured Wesleyanism at an earlier period but had turned to Whitefield's Calvinism in 1755, were at first in doubt about this major work of God, but were convinced on 13 July 1759 when they visited Everton and met the fifteen- or sixteen-year-old Alice Miller, 'the little pale girl who had been justified on the 20th of May'.

Madan and Romaine belonged to the slowly growing group of evangelical ministers with an Anglican background who rejected Wesley's secondary theology. They did not want any close alliance with Wesleyanism. They were moderate Calvinists and they distrusted talk about Christian perfection. In the mid-century search for a clearly defined national Protestantism, this reappearance of the Reformed rather than Lutheran tradition in the Church of England had two important outcomes. First, as at Everton, this new group protected what might be called primary Anglicanism, and so limited the attractiveness of Wesleyanism within the parish system. Second, evangelicalism endured, a powerful factor in the survival of Anglican institutions whose collapse was repeatedly foretold by 'well-informed observers'.

Finally, on 6 August 1759, Wesley himself visited Everton, where he also examined Alice Miller. She had fallen into a trance while hymnsinging was going on. 'I do not know whether I ever saw a human face look so beautiful,' he commented, though it should be added that this kind of description was common in such cases. She was unconscious for more than an hour, though speaking briefly and crying from time to time, then:

about seven her senses returned. I asked : 'Where have you been?' 'I have been with my saviour.' 'In heaven or in earth?' 'I cannot tell, but I was in glory.' 'Why then did you cry?' 'Not for myself but for the world; for I saw that they were on the brink of hell.' 'Whom did you desire to give glory to God?' 'Ministers, that cry aloud to the world; else will they be proud; and then God will leave them, and they will lose their own souls.'[49]

These are Wesley's own published comments on Everton, based on first-hand observation. Alice Miller's case underlines again the importance of women of all ages in what was happening. For the moment she was close to becoming a prophetess, because she satisfied the primary demand for evidence of contact with divine power. She was doing what Wesley and his colleagues were for various reasons unable to do – they were certainly not prophets, for example, and they did not go into trances – and therefore she could influence professionals like Madan and Romaine, and leave Wesley at least acquiescent.

There was a particular element in her testimony, which Wesley duly printed, which throws light on why neither the Anglican hierarchy nor parish priests were necessarily impressed by what they read or heard. This is the anticlerical theme, which one may assume had been fed to her by Berridge and others, and which was also reported (in a different form, but at first hand) from the neighbouring village of Triplow. There a woman was converted who had had, allegedly, 'nine or ten children by whoredom, and being at last married, [she found] her husband was more angry with her for hearing the word than he probably would have been for committing adultery. Nor was her minister displeased that she never came to church, but mightily strove to prevent both her and all the sinners of his parish from going to hear the gospel.'[50]

This kind of story, full of internal but not necessarily Dissenting resentment against the Anglican parochial ministry, recurs in various forms, and it would not be unfair to say that it was present in John Wesley's own clerical denunciations of the ministers of the established Church. This anticlericalism went deeper than opposition to the social and political power of the clergy, which increased steadily through the eighteenth century. Critics such as Alice Miller, an adolescent girl claiming to draw directly on supernatural authority, threw doubt on the religious competence of the clergy, and this in turn implies that eighteenth-century society was more sharply divided than it has been fashionable to assert in recent years. Not everyone in Hanoverian England thought that society was fundamentally bound together by Anglicanism. Many middling and much poorer people felt themselves to be living in different worlds from those inhabited by elites. Such people lived in subcultures of their own, in which they satisfied their primary religious needs, either by manipulating Christian institutions, or by inventing religious forms of their own.

There are two further significant sentences at the end of the story from Triplow: 'I observed also a beggar-girl, seven or eight years old, who had scarce any clothes but a ragged piece of old rug. She too had felt the word of God as a two-edged sword, and mourned to be covered with Christ's

righteousness.'[51] Whether the child understood phrases like
being 'covered with Christ's righteousness' we cannot know:
the narrator seems quite unconscious of the irony contained
in the bringing together of 'raggedness' and 'covered'. There
was a primary assumption, in any case, that the Spirit enabled
her to know – that she belonged to the cohorts of peasants,
women and children whose minds had been opened to supernatural truth. She may have recognised that there was anger
loose which she must propitiate. The child must have been
illiterate, she was probably hungry as well as cold, and the un-
restrained adult behaviour around her must have bewildered
her. The narrator's choice of this incident for relation implied
a reference to the familiar sentimental image conjured up by
the words 'a little child shall lead them', so that the fact that
she 'mourned' (she was, unsurprisingly, in tears) confirmed
the action of a divine power. The child is absorbed into a
vocabulary, made invisible by the ritual in which she was en-
veloped. What, if anything, they did with her is not reported,
but one is bound to translate this scene as the beggar-girl's des-
perate search for acceptance by any subculture which would
admit her and give her a human status in the form of shelter,
food and clothing. Eighteenth-century English society could
not change drastically, and at Everton, in the far from heavenly depths of the Cambridgeshire countryside, some of the
restraints which governed it can be glimpsed.

One may agree with Jonathan Clark that Hanoverian
Anglicanism should not simply be reduced to a reflection of
social forces; Anglicanism, as he says, was more than a figleaf
for possessive individualism or a code for the agenda of un-
derground radicalism.[52] The eighteenth-century Church was
not totally out of touch with the primary religious wants of its
membership, nor did it lack plausible theologies, both for those
who relied on what they believed to be Christian experience,

and also for those for whom religion had first and foremost to possess an acceptable intellectual basis. The Church of England had its faults: too many of the clergy had become obsessed with promotion and profit. Nevertheless, Anglicanism could satisfy some of the needs of primary religion through groups such as the Wesleyans and other evangelicals, and also preserve a plausible theology, even if Anglican and other intellectuals were nibbling at the foundations. One may also, just, agree with Clark that any practical alternative to the regime would have needed an alternative religious content, but this is more a political than a religious statement. Only warfare could have made Jacobite Catholicism a serious alternative. Remarkable as this may seem, the Anglican response to religious competition, to the efforts of the Wesleyans, the Friends, the Dissenters, the Unitarians and the Catholics to build up strong denominations, was adequate.

6

Conclusions

The general conclusions of this study are straightforward. There was no large-scale eighteenth-century evangelical revival which saved the soul of the British nation through the miraculous gift of the Spirit. What did happen was confined largely to the middle sectors of the population. There was no Church of the Industrial Revolution. The actual religious movements had two components. Primary religion, as I have defined it, found new outlets, at first inside and then outside the Church of England. From these developments there developed fresh institutions, which had more influence in the nineteenth century in subtly altered forms than they did in the eighteenth. Second, political Protestantism, which had been hardpressed by the Counter-Reformation in the seventeenth century when France was in the ascendant, recovered institutionally, militarily and (in the longer run) intellectually. In Europe, Prussia started its tragic march towards the rank of great power; Holland and the Baltic states retained their independence, and Britain expanded vigorously into the East and North America. The decisive event, however, was the emergence of the United States with a powerful Protestant culture, the direct ancestor of the modern Religious Right. (If Providence intended that, Providence succeeded.)

In Britain it has to be recognised that anti-Catholicism was more than just a crude mob reaction or irrational set of prejudices. Behind it, by the eighteenth century, lay more than two centuries of political, economic and military conflict, as well as intense differences in the understanding of the nature of human existence. British Protestantism became extremely unlike European Catholicism. British nationalism, harshly self-confident, inevitably reflected this as political and economic success affected the country's outlook. It was not the least of the achievements of Enlightenment and some Protestant thinking in the eighteenth century, in Europe as well as in Britain, to identify these passions as destructive, and to try to overcome them. The material factors which drove forward the creation of the first British empire, together with the Protestant recovery as a whole, did not halt the process of sceptical, scientific and historical thinking which had gone on ever since the Renaissance, side by side with the conflicts between the various forms of Christianity.

Liberal Protestantism put down strong roots in the eighteenth century, especially in the Church of England and in Dissent. Although the economic stability of the new Protestant movements, especially Wesleyanism, helps to explain the decline of primary religious activities in their ranks, it is also true that already in the eighteenth century liberal Protestantism acted as a check on those energies. This should not be neglected when we assess the importance of religious change in the eighteenth century, as though only transparent orthodoxy deserved the name of religion, and as though liberal religion could have no useful influence.

We must now turn to Wesleyanism itself, beginning with consideration of John Wesley. Uncertainty hangs over any description of John Wesley's character. He has to be looked at in the context of Wesleyanism, which grew out of the English past, incorporating Dissenting as well as Anglican tradition, and reflecting the country's social divisions. Above all, Wesleyanism offered a way in which some of those who were dissatisfied with their roles and opportunities in English society could alter their situation. There was a Wesleyan story about this, which even invoked the Holy Spirit as the author of the tale, and John Wesley's own more limited story was as much a Wesleyan as a personal invention. Nevertheless, strong personalities were involved, among them John Wesley himself, and an assessment of him is essential.

Naturally authoritarian, Wesley found in religion a means of imposing his will on some of his contemporaries, though rarely on his social equals. He withdrew in his late thirties from the polite, but not upper-class, Anglican society which he knew, and formed a counter-society on a religious basis which was more than marginal, though in later years he liked to imagine that the early societies had come from the poor, the dissolute and rejected. The bulk of his followers were in no sense always poor but they were rarely rich, many of them had long histories of religious anxiety and experiment, some against an Anglican and some against a Nonconformist background. They often suffered from deep self-dissatisfaction and they had not always settled the crisis brought on by adulthood.

Wesley shared the self-rejection and the problems of maturity. He retreated from Oxford University, where he felt powerless, and from his ill-starred mission to the American Colonies, where he pleased no one. His Moravian-type conversion in 1738, to which belief in the divine forgiveness of past errors and failings was central, enabled him to shift from the unending pursuit of self-discipline which had earned him and his Oxford friends the label of 'Methodists' to a more resilient discipline of faith. At this point he calmed his mind by adopting a theological explanation of the world, but the impact of the primary religious needs of the people who joined the societies intensified after the move to Bristol and deeply affected his personality. Within the compass of this expanding subculture he was able to believe what he wanted to believe, to tolerate and exploit in an approving community ideas about faith, healing, guidance and so forth, which he knew would encounter only very limited sympathy, and sometimes disdain, elsewhere. The pietist system assured him that faith could transform the natural man and woman.

Above all, Wesley was able to drop out of the mainstream of British society, to wander around the British Isles for about fifty years, in the firm and honest belief that he was specially called by God to behave in this way. The importance of this pilgrimage for Wesleyanism, as distinct from Wesley himself, should not be exaggerated. It is significant that:

in spite of John Wesley's twenty-six visits to Cumbria, the only important society established before his death was at Whitehaven, his favourite Cumbrian place and destination for the traveller on his frequent Irish crossings. There were a few small societies scattered across West Cumberland, and a promising beginning in Carlisle, but until the late eighteenth century Methodist membership was under 500 in the county . . . John Wesley was not happy or at home in rural areas, if only because he found their inhabitants lacking in education, emotion, and response to his outpourings.[1]

Wesley itinerated because he needed to itinerate.

When he was in his thirties he could not face a future which would consist of marrying a woman whom he thought was suitable to be a clergyman's wife and then spending his time in the repetitive activities of a country parish. Though sometimes attracted by particular women, he always viewed marriage with suspicion; but when in his middle-age those who thought they knew him best, including George Whitefield, insisted that he ought to marry, he did so, and then tried to apply the same combination of authoritarianism and providential drift to his new domestic situation. When the marriage to Mrs Vazeille failed he held her responsible.

If one takes this approach to Wesley, seeing him as caught up in a religious movement that he could not control as he wanted, the dominant elements in his life seem to have been his refusal to modify his initially pre-enlightenment cast of mind, and his dropping out at the social level, an act which was not the result of his intellectual withdrawal but the way in which he coped with his personal problems. He was not anti-intellectual, in the manner of some of the itinerants, but he did not question the classical, including biblical, authority on which his education had relied, and he made little theologically of the scientific advances of the late seventeenth century. Instead, his new religious environment became his standard of measurement. Once he had accepted the leading role in what became a Wesleyan subculture, his reactions to the unexpected religious experiences he encountered there hardened into a confident system.

This impression of a self-assured religious leader is not impaired by the letter he wrote to Charles Wesley in 1766 (see p. 30), where he talked about his comparative lack of ecstatic experience. Comparative, because one is bound to doubt that Wesley could seriously have thought that he had no ecstatic reactions at all. The *Journals* make clear that in the early years his role in the more exciting meetings of the societies was not that of a bystander taking notes, but of a commanding figure who guided the group towards a climax. When he stood at the centre of such waves of communal passion, stimulating and controlling them, as he certainly did, the Wesley of the *Journals* does not give the impression of being even slightly alienated. When he described these events he did not question what had happened, he defined and approved what took place as divinely prompted. He did not hesitate to use the language of perfect holiness to stir up others, he was always demanding that they 'go on to perfection', and he believed their claims that they had achieved a state of perfect love in which the self was possessed by a divine Spirit. That he did not talk about himself in the same fashion may have been partly because he was not neurotically bothered about his own moral situation: he was confident of the general correctness of his own actions, teaching and judgements. He had no rational fear of personal damnation.

Some commentators have suggested that Wesley comforted himself with the assurance of those Wesleyans who seemed to have no problems with the language of possession and perfection. Wesley certainly used their assertions as an apologist, but he wanted his own kind of blessing, and an instantaneously faith-healed and ethically transformed personality was not at the heart of what he wanted. In the letter to Charles he made no reference to the general experience of Wesleyanism, but professed: 'I never had any other proof of the eternal or invisible world than I have now; and that is none at all, unless such as fairly shines from reason's glimmering ray.'[2] Here he was expressing the deepest level of primary religious emotion, its passionate longing for signs, miracles, healings, certainties. He reminds one of John Henry Newman, also in retreat from Oxford, who wrote:

our first feeling is one of surprise and (I may say) of dismay, that His control of the world is so indirect, and His action so obscure. This is the first lesson that we gain from the course of human affairs. What strikes the mind so forcibly and so painfully is His absence (if I may so speak) from His own world. It is a silence that speaks. It is as if others had got possession of His works.[3]

Newman's answer to his uncertainties emerges as an appeal to his 'burdened conscience', which, he said, pronounced 'without any misgiving that God exists'.[4] This seems to have been Wesley's answer as well, when he claimed that the Spirit, like a light shining in their hearts, gave to the simple faith of peasants, women and children a knowledge of God which eluded the intellectual (see p. 172). The shift of ground is recognisably human, and in Newman's case it meant he could switch his mind back to doctrine and say that the appalling state of the world confirmed Roman Catholic teaching about the Fall. Of the two men Wesley was the more exposed, because he argued publicly at length that more than Newman's kind of intuitive moral certainty was possible, and could be possessed by faith. There was a wide gap between his 'reason's glimmering ray' and Newman's amazingly knowing conscience. Neither man was responding to the growing criticism of old authority: both wanted reassurance that intellectually, as well as emotionally, nothing had changed, or had to change.

This is one way of examining Wesley's personality. Another might start from the fact that he was the child of parents whose understanding of the world was wrapped up in religion. His father and mother, who were not happily married, were absorbed in a religio-political culture which disintegrated in their lifetime. One should not attach much importance to his failure to learn in the family a balanced attitude to women. On the one hand, Charles Wesley married successfully and worked hard to advance his sons' careers; on the other, John's tendency to regard women as instruments rather than personalities (instruments, that is, of either God or men), closely resembled the predominant eighteenth-century masculine pattern in English society. This patriarchal idea of women was not new, but it had been reinforced in the later seventeenth century, as the European worldview adjusted to, for example, the collapse of the astrological picture of the universe, and to Harvey's discovery of the circulation of the blood.[5] For a time the traditional masculine attitude to women hardened.

Wesley could conceive of existence only within a web of intense religious feelings and beliefs. As he grew up, leaving Lincolnshire for a London school, attending Oxford, spending time in the parishes of a few friends, and then trying Georgia, he could not find an equivalent of his family which would satisfy both mind and emotion. One realises why the communal pietism of the Moravians attracted him so much, and why he replicated it in many ways in his own societies. His mother, Susanna Wesley, may have been devoted to the Puritan and Lockean view that children's wills should be broken, but she failed with John. His upbringing strengthened his will. He applied the same educational theory himself at the boarding school he opened in Kingswood, near Bristol, and showed no curiosity about its consequences.

Wesley's family left him with certainties which were usually verbal, not visual. He does not, for example, report the kind of image of Jesus on the Cross which was not uncommon among the Wesleyans. He recorded some dreams, but left their meaning obscure. How far his search for the hand of God in events could go is shown by his habit of opening the Bible at random in the hope of finding guidance, and in the use of drawing lots to take difficult decisions, a custom which occurred among the Moravians, and which the Annual Conference briefly continued after his death. Looked at in this way, Wesley was strong-willed and ambitious, convinced of the centrality of a religious explanation of the world, patriarchal towards women, unimaginative and intellectually incurious, critical of his superiors and with little protection against the intrusive power of primary religion.

This is a harsh view, though Anglican commentators have tended to follow it. Later Methodist writers follow the line of Alexander Knox (1757–1831), a Northern Irishman who knew Wesley and approved of his holiness teaching. Knox's

Remarks on the Life and Character of John Wesley were written
in reply to the poet Robert Southey, a conservative Anglican
who had published a detailed, perceptive biography of Wesley
in 1820. Southey emphasised Wesley's ambition as well as his
inability to resist what the previous century had correctly
(in Southey's opinion) called vulgar enthusiasm. Knox would
allow only that Wesley:

> was always gratified by hearing or reading of illapses [half-faintings of
> religious excitement], or raptures, or supposed extraordinary manifes-
> tations, when he was assured of the moral rectitude of the party . . . but
> while he thus delighted in the soarings of others, he himself could not
> follow them in their flights: there was a firmness in his intellectual
> texture which would not bend to illusion. It was easy to deceive his
> reasoning faculty, but there was a soundness in his imagination which
> preserved him, personally, from all contagion of actual fanaticism.[6]

Knox was determined to protect Wesley against the charge
of fanaticism, and so constructed the implausible figure of a
man who delighted in other people's soaring religious flights,
whose firm intellect prevented him from bending to illusion
(though it was easy to deceive his reasoning faculty), and who
was nevertheless saved from contagion by a sound imagination. This confusion will not do. The necessary distinction
is not between fanaticism and a cool imagination. Wesley
stepped back from what he registered as excess, which is the
essence of fanaticism; but he accepted a wide range of phenomena as being inspired by God, and did not imagine that they
were excessive. That was the point of Southey's criticisms,
and Knox failed to find a way of turning the thrust aside.

If Wesley had not been personally convinced of the value
of many of the phenomena to which Knox was referring, he
could not have handled them in the way he did. He would
have had either to withdraw from the societies or to discipline
severely those who talked and behaved in this manner between

the 1730s and the 1770s. As we have seen, he never disavowed the claims to holiness made in London in the 1760s: what he deplored was the way in which his followers slipped back into normality. On the other hand, his assent to the occurrence of ecstatic feelings and extraordinary manifestations does not mean that one should use words such as fanaticism and vulgar enthusiasm. By Knox's time these were pejorative expressions intended to place the great part of Wesleyanism outside respectable religion. Wesley regarded what happened as biblically permissible, but not as unquestionable. What were characteristic were the long hesitations which often preceded his criticism, and the dogmatism with which, every now and again, he supported striking claims in print.

Knox believed in Wesley's doctrine of holiness, and it may have been Wesley's refusal to say that he had received the gift which made Knox refer to Wesley's power of detachment. There is no doubt that Wesley's spiritual condition puzzled the Wesleyans themselves, and that they enjoyed discussing it. There is a letter, dated 5 April 1750, from William Briggs to Wesley which throws light on these attitudes. Briggs (1722– c.88) was the son of an early eighteenth-century rector of Holt in north Norfolk. He associated with the Foundery Wesleyans from 1742, and as an itinerant had helped Grace Murray in Newcastle upon Tyne when she was depressed in 1744; he worked at the Custom House in London and was also John Wesley's Book Steward from 1753 to 1759. In this letter, which he wrote when he was about twenty-eight, he told Wesley that he thought Wesley:

had the knowledge of all Christian experience, but not the experience of all he knew . . . I think you find not abidingly a deep sense of your own spiritual weakness, the nearness of Christ to save, or a sweet communion with God by the Holy Ghost. You have the appearance of all Christian graces, but they do not I think spring from a deep experience or change of nature. [7]

These remarks are usually treated as no more than a candid view of Wesley's capacity for religion: they are docketed with Knox's judgement that Wesley 'would have been an enthusiast, if he could,' which begs the issue[8]. The two statements are used to explain his silence about the degree to which he shared in the ecstatic holiness movment which he advocated so consistently.

One is reminded of S. T. Coleridge's summary of the impression Wesley made on him as he was reading Southey's biography of the preacher. Coleridge deduced:

Wesley never rose above the region of logic and strong volition. The moment an idea presents itself to him, his understanding intervenes to eclipse it, and he substitutes a conception by some process of deduction. Nothing is immediate to him. Nor could it be otherwise, with a mind so ambitious, so constitutionally, if not a commanding, yet a ruling genius – i.e. no genius at all, but a height of talent with unusual strength and activity of individual will.[9]

Knox argued that Wesley had been saved by a streak of rationalism from the full effect of popular Wesleyanism. Coleridge, who, despite his later reputation for liberalism in religion, was a conservative Anglican who believed passionately that the religious consciousness of men and women provided the point of contact with the divine Spirit, thought that Wesley used his intellect to fence himself off from reality. Briggs argued that Wesley fell short of true communion with God – it is not a question of falling short only of perfect holiness – because of a lack of humility. Perhaps what one sees here is evidence that Wesley's exposure to primary religious forces gradually reduced his capacity to dominate his followers, to act as a spiritual director. He was right in not making claims about his own holiness, and to that extent was more humble than many of his associates; he should have gone further, and recognised that one should not use the prestige of experience to govern the minds of others, that there had come a time when everybody in the Wesleyan societies

was talking much too freely about love and holiness, about
Providence and humility.

In any case, Briggs's judgement was not impartial; his letter
formed part of an ongoing internal Wesleyan controversy.
The movement was new and small in 1750 and had no clear
future, but the size of such groups never precludes a struggle
for power. The possibility of Grace Murray, who was already
beginning to act as a religious leader, becoming Wesley's wife,
threatened the influence of others, and, whatever they might
say about holiness or Providence, they fought back. In this
letter Briggs complained to Wesley that he could not find 'that
deep union with [you] as I have with some.'[10] Briggs's words
should be read in the context of the whole letter, which went
on to discuss the way in which Charles Wesley had reacted to
the idea that John might marry Grace. Briggs, an old friend
of both Murray and Bennet, the other man in the dispute, had
opposed the marriage, and was now defending himself against
John's reproaches. He protested:

My thoughts are far from what you apprehend. I never once imagined
you quite fallen from grace, though I have sometimes been inclined
to think you had received loss. Much less did I ever think Mr Charles
quite in the right. I have ever thought he was an instrument in the
hands of God preventing an evil; though there was much evil in the
instrument. In his account I observed where he eyes the glory of God
[kept his attention fixed on things above] he spoke and acted with great
wisdom; but where pride and passion excited, his speech and behaviour
was raving; and perhaps through the whole there was more nature than
grace.[11]

The confidence with which Briggs could assure John that
Charles had been an instrument in the hands of Providence
suggests how slippery and overused this language had become.
Briggs felt entitled both to condemn John's intentions and to
declare that there was more nature than grace in Charles's

opposition. Yet Briggs was not an innocent commentator on what had happened. In fact, he and John Bennet had been in constant communication, and on 5 December 1749 Briggs had written to Bennet, confiding: 'I have lost all confidence in him [Wesley], and without a testimony of his humiliation can never esteem him again as I once did. But when God breaks that stubborn sinew in his neck, then shall I love him better than ever.'[12] Bennet had written back to Briggs on 3 March 1750. 'I have reason to think', he wrote, 'that the stubborn sinew in Mr [Wesley's] neck is broken, from several letters received of late from him.'[13] The reference to the stubborn sinew comes from Isaiah 48: 4, 'Because I knew that thou art obstinate, and thy neck is an iron sinew, and thy brow brass', and was aimed at Wesley's refusal to budge from the view that although Providence had not finally approved his marriage, this did not mean that Bennet's marriage to Grace Murray was itself the will of Providence.

Wesley wrote to Bennet on 3 November 1749: 'I was never yet convinced that your marriage was according to the will of God, or to speak more plainly, that it was at all consistent with justice, mercy, or truth. Nevertheless, I loved you tenderly both before and since, and had still an amazing confidence in you both.'[14] Bennet revealed that he had had a dream-cum-vision, which he naturally interpreted in his own favour, though Wesley inevitably thought that he had misinterpreted it.

There is a sharp contrast between the immaculate style of Wesley's formal defences of Wesleyan piety and theology, and the chaotic underside of the movement, in which a simpler version of religion prevailed, which affected the leaders themselves. The events of 1749, and the not dissimilar emotional struggles that followed John's marriage to Mrs Vazeille in February 1751, came at the end of Methodism's first decade, not at the end of its first few weeks. They involved those who claimed to have been thoroughly transformed by the converting power of God, and who adopted a superior tone to Wesley, as those who had got further along the road. The exchanges read like a domestic tragi-comedy set in a pietist community by an author with a clear eye for the limitations of practical, and primary, religion. It was not as easy as Wesley had assumed to transform human behaviour, or as wise as he had supposed to democratise the idea of holiness as a subjective state of consciousness and a pragmatically assessable pattern of conduct.

The implication – that the system had failed – brings us to the question of what Wesleyanism itself achieved. In the course of the eighteenth century the societies became a national body with a common subculture. This culture had its own fund of stories about itinerant and local preachers, about exciting meetings and successful revivals. Many of the itinerants were well known throughout the societies. The Sunday School movement was beginning to expand as an organ of self-education, albeit limited by the itinerants' resistance to the teaching of writing on a Sunday. Anti-slavery, and in some areas of the country anti-Catholicism, dominated the Wesleyan view of the world outside, but the world inside counted for almost everything.

There was division in that world. As Professor Langford has argued, in the eighteenth century 'the frontier of gentility ran through the centre of middle-class life, not so much dividing poor from rich or lower-class from upper, but rather separating small tradesmen and householders from more opulent business and professional men'.[15] This was very true within Wesleyanism, and helps to explain the tensions which could arise between the itinerants on the one hand and the local preachers, Sunday School teachers and class-leaders on the other. Local preachers often felt they were entitled to do whatever an itinerant did, and were happy to baptise their own children. The local trustees of Connexional property were inclined to believe they owned their chapels and were jealous of the itinerants' authority. Some Sunday schools operated outside the system altogether. The Moravians had suggested that the best form of the Christian congregation was a self-supporting colony in the heart of a fallen world. The Wesleyan society never withdrew as far from social power as the Moravian example entailed, but the Wesleyans had the same sense of being unique and apart. Many of the members exhibited an upwardly mobile personality, which developed as a result of hard work, self-examination, self-discipline, and sometimes by the cleansing but temporary loss of identity in a common will.

The goal was not holiness but respectability, a word easily misunderstood as the quintessence of Victorianism, and interpreted as involving hypocrisy. Yet in this case respectability meant genuine, hard-won moral and financial stability, not attained in the form of an idealised peasant farmer who lives off his own on his own piece of land, but in the midst of stressful, expanding towns and cities like Leeds and Manchester, or isolated, danger-ridden and hard-drinking mining communities in the South-West and the North-East, which were constantly in need of domestication, mutual trust and peacefulness. These were people who did not think of morality in terms of an ascetic negation of the self, but who valued an honest, unostentatious style of life.[16]

The Wesleyan societies seem to have lacked intellectual curiosity and aesthetic pleasure; only the enjoyment of music, which never died out, compensated for this. As John Rule has written: 'Methodism poses one of the most difficult questions to answer for "social control" theory in which the forces of pressure are seen as a successful *external* imposition of middle-class values upon the working-classes. In fact, we have to explain a cultural divide which split the working classes themselves and which was as significant in separating the "roughs" from the "respectables" as was the "imperialism" of other classes.'[17] This is truer of the nineteenth than of the eighteenth century: from my point of view the Wesleyanism of the 1740s and 1750s was very much an Anglican experiment in 'social control'. When that experiment failed, Wesleyanism moved much closer to the Dissenting model of the 'gathered' community. One does not have to think of this as a social tragedy, prevention of the birth of a potential beauty.

The next question is to what extent the women who became members of the eighteenth- and early nineteenth-century societies felt their lives were enhanced by their experience. Wesleyan men certainly accepted the conventions and habits of a male-dominated society, as can be seen in the attitudes of Charles and John Wesley to Grace Murray, whom they treated as someone who should obey and provide. After twenty years of marriage John Wesley still took it for granted that Mrs Vazeille would help him with money for projects such as the Book Room and the school at Kingswood. Professor Barker-Benfield has argued that Wesleyan women, and to a lesser extent, men, shared in the eighteenth-century cult of sensibility.[18] For example, Wesleyans scorned fashionable clothes and dressed austerely, much as in sentimental fiction characters went in for pastoral simplicity. Both groups condemned politicians and wealthy aristocrats for corruption and ambition. Men and women gave vent to their feelings through tears, sighs, groans, tremblings, and faintings, both religious and sentimental.

Even more significant was the practice of prison visiting. When John Cennick, for instance, was in Haverfordwest in

May 1753, he went to see Edward Lee, who was in prison for theft and had been sentenced to death. Cennick converted Lee before his execution, and the sheriff and others were more than willing to join in what became a parade through the streets to the gallows. Lee willingly accepted that he deserved his hanging.[19] The feelings seem sincere, but the drama made out of the execution is repulsive in modern Western eyes, though socially acceptable at the time, and recalls the satisfaction, evidently sexual in part, with which Boswell accompanied prisoners to their deaths in London.[20]

Barker-Benfield plays down religious attitudes in comparison with a cult of sensibility which she believes affected the position of women. Wesleyan preaching and writing attached a new value to women within the societies, not as creatures of feeling but as vehicles of the Spirit. This did not extend their freedom intellectually, and the social change was marginal. If some women developed a new opinion of themselves, part of the explanation may lie in the growth of cities like Leeds, Manchester, Newcastle and London, in which size and the jarring of wealth and poverty caused a loosening of bonds, a revision of relationships.

The city, however, was not the only place where women behaved differently. Let us look at Cennick once more, writing on 29 October 1743:

Not long after this Sister Ann Beaker followed the other souls who in this season went to the marriage of the Lamb. She was first awakened when I preached at Castle Coombe and remained athirst for redemption till after the next Christmas, when it pleased the Holy Ghost to glorify the Son of Man before her in his bloody form, it was so as if he stood before her with all his wounds and bid her put her finger into the nailpoints and thrust her hand into his side and not be faithless but believing. This was so felt in her heart with divine power that she cried out, My Lord and my God. She continued henceforward in love with her eternal husband.

Ann Beaker died of smallpox, single, at the age of about twenty-two. Her vision happened in Wiltshire, in a rural society where you would not expect a cult of sensibility, and she found herself redeemed (rather than reconstructed) in pietist language to be the bride of the Lamb. There was no question of modifying patriarchy, but all the same something had shifted here, and would be picked up again early in the following century when the Primitive Methodists broke into the Wiltshire countryside. One must not ignore the possibilities of individual transformation.

On two fronts Wesleyanism achieved little by the end of the eighteenth century. First, the societies gave up the attempt to sustain a holiness movement at its heart. It was left to American revivalists, most of them Methodist, to go on preaching holiness in the United States, and they brought the doctrine back to England in the 1840s (Charles Finney and James Caughey), the 1860s (James Caughey again and Phoebe Palmer), and the 1870s (the Pearsall Smiths), though never with more than slight success, and that as much in evangelical Anglican as in Wesleyan circles. It is a law that American revivalists do not revive English religion. Individuals might be affected, but neither Moody and Sankey in the later nineteenth century, Torrey and Alexander at the opening of the twentieth, nor Billy Graham after the Second World War halted the overall decline in church membership that began in the Victorian period despite the efforts of Finney, Caughey and Palmer. The marginalisation of holiness may have involved an intellectual or existential tragedy for the few, but it hardly affected the majority, who had been living without reference to the holiness ideology for at least a generation.

Second, and much earlier, Wesleyanism stopped trying to function as a pietist reforming movement inside the Church of England. The positive results had been few. At first there were signs that lay Anglicans might accept the restoration of the kind of moral and spiritual discipline which Wesley and other parsons aimed at by means of the societies. Theoretically, these local Wesleyan communities might have been able to influence what happened in the parish church, but there is not much evidence of interaction. Wesleyans who preferred to think of themselves as Anglicans survived in some areas until John Wesley's death, but then the few thousand who remained melted back into the Establishment, because they wanted to receive holy communion from an Anglican parson, not from the itinerants, who now took the power to administer the sacrament into their own hands. Institutionally, the two bodies moved steadily away from one another.

Finally, what was the political importance of the Wesleyan Societies? A new social bloc formed, which at first seemed to add to the power of Dissent. Wesley's support for the Crown in both the Jacobite rebellion and the American War of Independence, together with his relentless attacks on the Moravians and Calvinists, helped to separate the Wesleyans from the Dissenters. He refused to back Lord George Gordon's appeal for violence in the London anti-Catholic riots of 1780, but he publicly opposed any change in the legal status of Catholics (a change which had become government policy), on the ground that they could not be trusted to keep faith with heretics, and so should not be treated as full citizens. In addition, he made it his business to visit Gordon in prison, and these policies won him the sympathy of many of the itinerants and laity.[21] Wesleyan interest in parliamentary reform was slight, and during the troubles in the factory areas during the French Revolutionary Wars the Wesleyan leaders firmly refused to help any of their members who became involved.

Nevertheless, Nicholas Rogers has suggested that in the 1780s 'evangelicalism was politically protean, part of a broader middle-class reform movement preoccupied with moral rectitude and the elimination of vice and corruption'.[22] Mary E. Fissell, writing with Bristol's mid eighteenth-century charitable institutions in mind, takes a similar view: 'A belief in the moral uses of incarceration, of the need to reform the manners of the poor, made charity and poor relief virtually identical. So too in their intention to found redemptive communities embodying the ideals of a primitive church, reformers who created workhouses and hospitals owed as much to inward religion as to philanthropy.'[23]

As far as the poor were concerned, writers on morals, economics and religion all stressed that the lower groups in eighteenth-century society had an obligation to work. They were not denied the status of human beings, or necessarily refused medical treatment; they might be trained for some kind of labour and given some education. They were included in the nation, as long as they worked and contributed to it. Religion was offered them as instruction and commandments. The primary offence was idleness, the aggravated offence was beggary, the criminal offence was theft. They had no business to get drunk, to riot, or, in the case of the women, to have children when unmarried. To the extent that Rogers's statement is true, Wesleyanism was an important component of a loose evangelical coalition, but the Wesleyans had only limited ideas about political action as such.

Nevertheless, one should not underrate the importance of what Wesleyan moralism did for a significant group of men and women. One eighteenth-century critic seems to have grasped the point, though he did not mention the Wesleyans by name. In *The Wealth of Nations* (1776) Adam Smith, himself a deeply convinced deist who disapproved of allowing any political power to religious bodies, described the tremendous difference which moving from the country to the town made on an ordinary person. Where he came from he was known and his conduct was watched. 'But as soon as he comes into a great city he is sunk in obscurity and darkness', and might lose his moral self altogether. 'He never emerges so effectually from this obscurity, his conduct never excites so much the attention of any respectable society, as by his becoming the member of a small religious sect.' Within a group bound together by an austere code of morals which, as Smith put it, might be rather disagreeably rigorous and unsocial, he could recover himself. This was what eighteenth-century Wesleyanism, adding its own style of religious sensibility, achieved for a large number of men and women.

Notes

I

1. C. Haydon, S. Taylor, J. Walsh (eds.), *The Church of England 1689–1833: from Toleration to Tractarianism* (Cambridge, 1993), p. 26. The quotation comes from the introductory essay, 'The Church and Anglicanism in the "long eighteenth century"', which both editors signed. The book tends to reflect the Anglican view that Wesleyanism happened outside the Church of England.

2. Belief in evil spirits did not die out rapidly in England after the Reformation. It was held for some time that Protestant ministers might entreat, but certainly not command, God to remove diabolic powers. This procedure was effectively ruled out by Canon 72 of the Church of England Canons of 1604. The Nonconformists asserted both the possibility of demonic possession and of fasting and prayer as remedies until the end of the seventeenth century. As long as the biblical text dominated Protestant thinking, Anglicanism could not rule out the notion of active evil spirits altogether.

3. Thomas Jackson (ed.), *The Lives of the Early Methodist Preachers* (London, 1846), vol. II, p. 173.

4. Ibid., p. 141.

5. Ibid., p. 190.

6. Ibid., pp. 191–2.

7. Ibid., pp. 272–3.

8. Harris (1714–73) was a Welsh Anglican who preferred Whitefield to the Wesleys, and became the founder of the Welsh Calvinist Methodists.

9 Cennick's papers are at Moravian Church House in Muswell Hill, London. This passage comes from his personal account of the preaching tour, p. 3.

10 Ibid., pp. 3–4.

11 Ibid., p. 4.

12 Piette was a French Catholic scholar who published *La réaction de John Wesley dans l'évolution protestante* (Brussels, 1925), translated as *John Wesley in the Evolution of Protestantism* (London, 1937). The English title fails to reflect Piette's view that Wesley was reacting against eighteenth-century Protestantism in a Catholic direction.

13 Ibid., p. 6.

14 Butler's *The Analogy of Religion* was published in 1736; I have used the Oxford edition of 1874.

15 Ibid., p. 263.

16 Joseph Priestley, 'An Examination of Mr Hume's Dialogues on Natural Religion (1780)', in *Hume on Natural Religion*, ed. S. Tweyman (Bristol, 1996), p. 90.

17 *Minutes of the Methodist Conferences* (London, 1862), p. 60.

18 Jonathan Clark, *Samuel Johnson, Literature, Religion and English Cultural Politics from the Restoration to Romanticism* (Cambridge, 1994), pp. 172–6.

19 See D. Hempton, M. Hill, *Evangelical Protestantism in Ulster Society 1740–1890* (London, 1992).

20 The French Prophets were Huguenot refugees who fled to England from Catholic persecution in the opening years of the century; they prophesied the imminent return of Christ, spoke in tongues and practised spiritual healing.

21 See D. Spadafora, *The Idea of Progress in Eighteenth-Century Britain* (New Haven, 1990), p. 95.

2

1 Wesley published groups of sermons, which he intended to function as theological guides for preachers and people.

2 A. C. Outler (ed.), *The Works of John Wesley*, ed. (Nashville, 1984), vol. I, pp. 434–5.

3 Ibid., p. 438.

4 Ibid., p. 442.

5 John Telford (ed.), *The Letters of John Wesley* (London, 1931), vol. V, pp. 15–16. Telford was the first to publish this letter, which has not been fully accommodated into the modern image of Wesley.

6 Selina, countess of Huntingdon (1707–91) became a Calvinist in 1739 and slowly set up a network of nearly a hundred proprietary chapels, each with an Anglican minister, technically her chaplain. She broke with the Church of England in 1781 and formed her own Connexion, more loosely structured than Wesley's. Her social position, and the location of her chapels in cities such as Bath and Brighton, gave her some influence on the development of eighteenth-century Calvinism.

7 Ibid., vol. V, pp. 188–9.

8 Ibid., vol. V, p. 185.

9 Fiona Macarthy, *William Morris* (London, 1994), p. 481.

10 Martin Schmidt, *John Wesley: A Theological Biography*, trans. Denis Inman (London, 1973), vol. II, Part 2, p. 172.

11 Ibid., pp. 172–3.

12 See E. G. Rupp, *Religion in England 1688–1791* (London, 1986), p. 385.

13 V. H. H. Green, *John Wesley* (London, 1964), p. 141.

14 See Linda Colley, *Britons, Forging the Nation 1707–1837* (London, 1992), especially pp. 11–54.

15 The Awakenings are dealt with in *Revivals, Awakenings and Reform*, W. G. McLoughlin (Chicago, 1978) and in *Colonial British America*, ed. J. P. Greene, J. R. Pole (Baltimore, 1984).

16 David Hume, *Treatise of Human Nature*, ed. L. A. Selby-Bigge (Oxford, 1941), p. 409.

17 See J. Kent, *Holding the Fort: Studies in Victorian Revivalism* (London, 1978) and R. Carwardine, *Transatlantic Revivalism 1790–1865* (Westport, Connecticut, 1978).

18 See Jonathan Clark, *English Society 1688–1832* (Cambridge, 1985).

19 In our own times, in Buenos Aires, Argentina, in 1998, pilgrims went to the local shrine of Cajetan, who had died in Naples in 1547, because he had the reputation there of being able to find jobs for the unemployed. See a report in the *Suddeutsche zeitung*, 8/9 August 1998.

20 John Skinner, *The Journal of a Somerset Rector 1803–34*, ed. H. and P. Coombs (Oxford, 1971).

21 G. Holmes, D. Szechi (eds.), *The Age of Oligarchy: Preindustrial Britain 1722–1783* (London, 1993), p. 115.

22 Van A. Harvey, *Feuerbach and the Interpretation of Religion* (London, 1995), p. 13.

23 F. Baker (ed.), *The Works of John Wesley, Letters 1740–1755* (Oxford, 1982), vol. XXVI, p. 4. The biblical reference is to Hebrews 6: 5.

24 See, for example, M. A. Noll et al. (eds.), *Evangelicalism: Comparative Studies of Popular Protestantism in North America, the British Isles and Beyond, 1700–1990* (London, 1994) and W. R. Ward, *The Protestant Evangelical Awakening* (London, 1992).

25 Telford, *Letters of John Wesley*, vol. VI, p. 61. The date was 28 December 1773.

26 Foote (1720–77) was a savage stage caricaturist. See also A. M. Lyles, *Methodism Mocked: the Satiric Reaction to Methodism in the Eighteenth Century* (London, 1960), a very sensible survey of the topic.

27 See R. E. Sullivan, *John Toland and the Deist Controversy* (Cambridge, Mass., 1982). Toland (1670–1722) became a pantheist, but he strongly advocated the idea of a civic religion.

28 Ann Bermingham, John Brewer (eds.), *The Consumption of Culture 1600–1800* (London, 1997), p. 344.

29 Nicholas Temperley, 'Music in Church', in H. D. Johnstone (ed.), *Music in Britain: the Eighteenth Century* (London, 1990), pp. 357–96. William Billings lived from 1746 to 1800.

30 O. A. Beckerlegge, F. Hildebrandt (eds.), *The Works of John Wesley, A Collection of Hymns for the use of the People called Methodists* (London, 1983), vol. VII, pp. 736, 766–9. Wesley appealed to the opinions of John Christopher Pepusch (1667–1752), whom the Wesleys knew; he came to England from Berlin about 1700, specialised in musical history and taught at the Charterhouse from 1737. Both Charles Burney (1726–1814) and John Hawkins (1719–89), the leading English music historians of the period, dismissed the claims made for Greek music.

31 Ibid., p. 506.

32 Ibid., pp. 563–4.

33 Ibid., pp. 561–2. The line 'I have now obtained the power' refers to Acts 1: 8, and the last line to I John 3: 9. The 'second blessing' is a term occasionally used by Wesley to indicate the gift of perfect holiness, which was 'second' in that it came after justification. The term had a dubious theological life of its own in parts of the nineteenth-century holiness movement, but that does not affect the meaning here.

34 H. D. Rack, *Reasonable Enthusiast: John Wesley and the Rise of Methodism* (London, 1989), pp. 400–1.

35 The *Christian Library* was published by Wesley during the first generation of Wesleyanism; it contained fifty volumes. Among the authors were Roman Catholic mystics such as Fenelon and Molinos, neither of whom has ever been quite persona grata in Rome. Many Anglican and Nonconformist writers featured in the *Library*, which Wesley edited from his own theological point of view. He claimed that overall he lost money through publishing the Library.

36 C. King, D. Ryscamp (eds.), *Letters and Prose Writings of William Cowper* (London, 1979), vol. I, pp. 565–6.

3

1 *Minutes of the Methodist Conferences* (London, 1862), p. 52.

2 Antinomianism, which dogged Protestantism from the sixteenth century, asserted that Christians were not bound by the moral law. ('To the pure all things are pure,' according to Titus 1: 15). Wesley constantly claimed that Calvinists were in danger of taking their assumed election to salvation as a liberation from ethical restraint. In practice, eighteenth-century English Calvinists usually took an austere moral line.

3 In lined-out singing a precentor read one, two or more lines of a hymn before the congregation sang them. The custom began in the seventeenth century, because many people could not read, and lasted well into the nineteenth in Britain and America. It was not specifically Wesleyan, and could produce a dirgelike effect.

4 See Mary Ransome (ed.), *Wiltshire Returns to Visitation Enquiries 1783* (Wiltshire Record Society, 1972). The bishop of Salisbury

at the time was Shute Barrington. As the work of Clive Field has shown, records are generally more useful for nineteenth- than eighteenth-century Wesleyanism.

5 For Zinzendorf (1700–60), see W. R. Ward, *Faith and Faction* (London, 1993), especially chapters 6–8.

6 Rowland Hill (1744–1833) supported Whitefield; ordained as a curate in 1773, he moved to the Surrey chapel in London in 1783. His brother Richard (1732–1808) was a not very successful evangelical M. P. from 1780 to 1806.

7 'Lukins was violently convulsed upon the exorcists singing a hymn, and the voices of various invisible agents proceeded from his mouth uttering horrible blasphemies.' See John Latimer, *The Annals of Bristol in the Eighteenth Century* (Bristol, 1893), pp. 483–4. A Yatton surgeon claimed that Lukins had been pretending to be bewitched for many years.

8 Horace Walpole, *Correspondence*, ed. W. S. Lewis (Yale, 1961), vol. XXXI, p. 276.

9 Ibid., p. 280.

10 Ibid., pp. 283–4. The minister whom More had refused to see was the Reverend Joseph Easterbrook, of the Temple church. He died in 1791.

11 Michael Macdonald, *Mystical Religion: Madness, Anxiety and Healing in Seventeenth-Century England* (Cambridge, 1981).

12 John Wesley, *The Works of John Wesley, Sermons on Several Occasions*, ed. A. C. Outler (Nashville, 1984), vol. I, pp. 682–5.

13 See J. Kent, 'Wesleyan Membership in Bristol 1783', in *An Ecclesiastical Miscellany* (Bristol and Gloucestershire Archaeological Society, 1976), pp. 105–32. The Membership Book for 1783–6 is bound in vellum covers, quarto size, and is in the possession of the New Room, Bristol. The handwriting is that of John Wesley.

14 The Poll Book is held by the Bristol City Library.

15 John Wesley, *The Works of John Wesley* (London, 1865), vol. XI, pp. 148–9. This comes from a brief public letter entitled 'How far is it the duty of a Christian minister to preach politics?'

16 T. Koditschek, *Class Formation in Urban Industrial Society in Bradford 1750–1850* (Cambridge, 1990).

17 Most of these papers are now available in volume 8 of Archbishop Secker's papers in the Lambeth Palace Library.

18 Lavington published in two instalments: vols. I and II (London, 1749); vol. III (London, 1751). The folio numbers run between 24 and 126.

19 See J. W. Reed (ed.), *Boswell: Laird of Auchinleck, 1778–1782* (New York, 1977), pp. 296–7. The Club met in a tavern. The problem with routs was the broad range of people who might be expected to attend them. The theatre was also viewed with suspicion because prostitutes often worked there.

20 Thomas Jackson (ed.), *The Lives of the Early Methodist Preachers* (London, 1846), vol. I, p. 181.

21 The *Arminian Magazine* was begun in 1778, its title changing to *The Methodist Magazine* in 1798. As the first name suggests, Wesley wanted to push the idea of the universal offer of salvation, in opposition to the Calvinists, but the itinerant contributors were also encouraged to stress the value of the holiness teaching.

22 A. M. Lyles, *Methodism Mocked: the Satiric Reaction to Methodism in the Eighteenth Century* (London, 1960), p. 18. Wesleyanism ceased to be a principal target of satire after 1800: evangelicalism (both Dissenting and Anglican) was then attacked steadily, not least by novelists such as Dickens.

23 A. C. Outler (ed.), *The works of John Wesley* (Nashville, 1984), vol. II, pp. 682–5.

24 Jackson, *Lives*, vol. II, pp. 327–8.

25 Ibid., vol. I, pp. 280–1.

26 Ibid., vol. II, p. 262. 'Seal' was another significant word, to be found, for instance, in I Corinthians 9: 2, where Paul told his readers: 'the seal of mine apostleship are ye'.

27 Ibid., vol. II, p. 262. Compare Revelation 12: 2: 'cried, travailling in birth'.

28 Ibid., vol. II, p. 216.

29 See J. Kent, *Holding the Fort: Studies in Victorian Revivalism* (London, 1978), pp. 25–7.

30 Jackson, *Lives*, vol. II, p. 216.

31 Ibid., p. 278.

32 Ibid., vol. I, p. 431.

33 Ibid., vol. I, p. 106.

34 Ibid., vol. I, p. 60.

35 See B. Semmel, *The Methodist Revolution* (London, 1974), pp. 70–9. Semmel translated the Wesleyan-Arminian stress on theological freedom much too easily into a radical political doctrine. What is most obvious about Alexander Kilham and the New Connexion in the 1790s is the absence of direct reference to the politics of the period in their propaganda.

36 S. T. Kimbrough, O. A. Beckerlegge (eds.), *The Unpublished Poetry of Charles Wesley* (Nashville, 1988), p. 153.

37 Ibid., pp. 98ff.

38 Ibid., p. 99.

4

1 See K. Morgan, 'Methodist Testimonials . . .', in J. Barry, K. Morgan (eds.) *Reformation and Revival in Eighteenth-Century Bristol* (Bristol Record Society, 1994), pp. 75–104, for the full texts. My comments on this material are my own.

2 In Wesley's last years a small number of women reached a quasi-independent status, but this situation ended with his death.

3 Compare, for example, I Corinthians, 2. 16: 'We have the mind of Christ.'

4 See S. Maitland, W. Mulford, *Virtuous Magic: Women Saints and their Meanings* (London, 1997).

5 A. Leger, *John Wesley's Last Love* (London, 1910), p. 67.

6 Ibid., p. 69. The basic reference is to Hebrews 3: 4.

7 Nothing is known about Elizabeth Halfpenny apart from this description of her religious experience. There was only one Halfpenny family in Bristol from *c.* 1728 to 1755, that of William Halfpenny, who may have been a Yorkshireman, and who called himself an architect; he did design buildings in Bristol. (I owe this information to O. J. Kent.)

8 Morgan, 'Methodist Testimonials . . . ', p. 92.

9 Ibid., p. 92.

10 Ibid., p. 93.

11 Ibid., p. 94.

12 Ibid., p. 92.

13 Felicity Nussbaum, *The Autobiographical Subject: Gender and Ideology in Eighteenth-Century England* (Baltimore, 1989), p. 179.

14 According to the editors, she may have been the wife of Thomas Sayce, a Bristol hooper, whom John Wesley stayed with in 1739–41.

15 Morgan, 'Methodist Testimonials . . .', p. 95.

16 Ibid., p. 97.

17 Ibid., p. 98.

18 Ibid., p. 101.

19 Ibid., p. 102.

20 Ibid., p. 103.

21 Ibid., p. 105.

22 N. Curnock (ed.), *John Wesley's Journal* (London, 1909–16, reprinted 1938), vol. III, pp. 197–8.

23 John Wesley borrowed the idea of bands from the Moravians. A band, of five to ten people, was smaller than the more relaxed class meeting, and meant to be more intense. Men, women, the married and the single met in separate bands once a week, confessed their sins and prayed for one another. Critics regarded bands as the Catholic confessional in another form.

24 Morgan, 'Methodist Testimonials . . .', p. 98.

25 Norman Fiering, *Moral Philosophy at Seventeenth-Century Harvard: a Discipline in Transition* (Chapel Hill, 1981), p. 320. Fiering's excellently written study draws a parallel between modern psychiatry and theological action on the soul.

26 It is interesting to compare his development with that of John Henry Newman, who willingly accepted the cult of saints, the use of relics, and the Counter-Reformation magnification of the image of the Virgin Mary, all of which were aspects of the same primary religious attitudes working in a Roman Catholic environment.

27 In *The Protestant Evangelical Awakening* (London, 1992) Ward suggests that Protestant revivalism did well as long as the laity directed events, but stagnated when the professional ministry took charge. He thinks that pietism grew partly as a lay protest against the early signs of the modern police-state. I suspect that pietism was itself one of the early signs of the police-state, to the extent that it encouraged informing on one's neighbours.

28 Leger, *John Wesley's Last Love*. The text was properly edited only in the twentieth century. Wesley continued the story up to

Grace Murray's decision to marry John Bennet; Leger also printed a twenty-seven-stanza verse account of the relationship written by Wesley. Leger added a full-scale discussion of both Murray's and Wesley's characters.

29 Ibid., p. 20.
30 Ibid., p. 21
31 Ibid., p. 24.
32 Ibid., p. 27.
33 Ibid., p. 34.
34 Ibid., p. 36
35 Ibid., p. 36.
36 George Cheyne, *Treatise on Health and Long Life* (London, 1725), pp. 122–4.
37 Leger, *John Wesley's Last Love*, p. 42.
38 Ibid., p. 45.
39 Ibid., p. 48.
40 Ibid., p. 102.
41 Ibid., p. 103.
42 Ibid., p. 50.
43 Ibid., pp. 50–1.
44 Ibid., p. 53. Italics in the original.
45 Ibid., pp. 53–6. Edward Perronet (1721–92) was the grandson of a French Protestant refugee; originally sympathetic to Wesley, he ended up as the minister of an Independent church in Canterbury. His father, Vincent (1693–1785), was vicar of Shoreham from 1728; he became one of Wesley's assistants in 1747 and worked closely with him for many years, opposing any move towards separation from the Church of England.
46 Ibid., p. 34.
47 David Lehmann, in his *The Struggle for the Spirit* (London 1996), pp. 139–42, gives a powerful acount of such a service in the Universal Church Pentecostalist building in Salvador.
48 Leger, *John Wesley's Last Love*, p. 103.
49 Ibid., p. 104.
50 Ibid., p. 105.
51 Ibid., pp. 70–2.
52 Ibid., p. 73.
53 Ibid., p. 65.

54 Ibid., p. 68.
55 Ibid., p. 83.
56 Ibid., p. 87.
57 Ibid., pp. 85–6.
58 Ibid., p. 14.
59 Ibid., pp. 94–5.

5

1 Thomas Hobbes, *Leviathan*, ed. W. G. P. Smith (Oxford, 1947), pp. 526–7.
2 Ibid., p. 360.
3 Ibid., p. 62.
4 Ibid., pp. 249–50.
5 Ibid., p. 469.
6 See an article by F. Dreyer, 'Faith and Experience in the Thought of John Wesley', in *The American Historical Review*, 1983, pp. 12–30, and R. E. Brantley, *Locke, Wesley and the Method of English Romanticism* (Florida, 1984). Also Rack, *Reasonable Enthusiast: John Wesley and the Rise of Methodism* (London, 1989), pp. 384–7.
7 John Spurr, *The Restoration of the Church of England, 1645–1689* (Yale, 1991), p. 307.
8 Ibid., p. 325. The words quoted are those of Isaac Barrow (1630–77), famous as a controversialist and admirer of Isaac Newton.
9 Fiering, *Moral Philosophy at Seventeenth-Century Harvard: a Discipline in Transition* (Chapel Hill, 1981), pp. 203–4.
10 Edmund Gibson, *Charge* (London, 1747), p. 4. Gibson (1669–1748) was an authority on Anglican law and custom who repeatedly challenged both Whitefield and Wesley on their conduct.
11 G. R. Cragg (ed.), *The Works of John Wesley* (Oxford, 1975), vol. XI, pp. 349–50.
12 Richard Graves, *The Spiritual Quixote*, ed. Clarence Tracey (London, 1967), p. 294.
13 Ibid., p. 294.
14 Ibid., p. 14.
15 *Observations on the Conduct and Behaviour of a certain Sect usually distinguished by the Name of Methodist*, published anonymously

(London, 1744). There seems to be no reasonable doubt that Gibson was the author.

16 Two other novelists should be mentioned: Laurence Sterne, (1713–68), who was so much the cleric sui generis that he virtually ignored Methodism; and Tobias Smollett (1721–71), whose *Humphrey Clinker*, published in the year of the author's death, portrayed, not unfairly, the eccentricities of a Methodist servant, from the point of view of Smollett's own tough medical secularity.

17 Samuel Richardson, *Sir Charles Grandison*, ed. Jocelyn Harris (London, 1986), vol. IV, p. 379.

18 Ibid., pp. 249–50.

19 Ibid., vol. VI, p. 22.

20 See John Beresford's selection from the diary, *Woodeford* (London, 1935).

21 Secker's cabinet of papers can be consulted at Lambeth Palace Library. This passage comes from f. 81.

22 See E. Radner, *The End of the Church: a Pneumatology of Christian Division in the West* (Michigan, 1998), p. 109.

23 Marguerite-Marie Alacoque (1647–90) popularised devotion to the heart of Mary as well as to the heart of Jesus. She and Eudes were both canonised in the 1920s.

24 Secker, f. 81.

25 Ibid., f. 82.

26 Ibid., f. 83.

27 Ibid., f. 84.

28 Ibid., f. 85.

29 Ibid., f. 85.

30 Ibid., f. 90.

31 Ibid., f. 86.

32 E. G. Rupp, *Religion in England 1688–1791* (Oxford, 1986).

33 Cragg, *Works of John Wesley*, vol. XI, p. 474.

34 Conyers Middleton, *Free Enquiry into the Miraculous Powers which are supposed to have existed in the Christian Church through several successive Ages* (Oxford, 1748).

35 Leslie Stephen, *History of English Thought in the Eighteenth Century* (London, 1963), p. 310.

36 John Wesley, *A Letter to the Bishop of Gloucester*, 1763, in Cragg, *Works of John Wesley*, vol. XI, p. 534.

37 Ibid., pp. 535–6.

38 Ibid., p. 515.

39 Ibid., p. 518.

40 D. Vasey (ed.), *The Diary of Thomas Turner 1754–1765* (Oxford, 1984).

41 Ibid., p. 125.

42 Ibid., p. 227.

43 N. Curnock (ed.), *John Wesley's Journal* (London, 1909–16, reprinted 1938), vol. IV, p. 331.

44 Ibid., p. 347.

45 Ibid., p. 337.

46 Ibid., p. 335.

47 Ibid., p. 347.

48 Ibid., p. 341.

49 Ibid., p. 347.

50 Ibid., p. 341.

51 Ibid., p. 341.

52 Jonathan Clark, *Samuel Johnson: Literature, Religion and English Cultural Politics from the Restoration to Romanticism* (Cambridge, 1994).

6

1 J. Burgess, 'The Growth and development of Methodism in Cumbria . . .', in *Northern History* (1981–82), vols. XVII–XVIII, pp. 137–8. Significantly, Wesleyanism outside the urban areas grew in 'outcast' communities such as those of the coalminers of Kingswood, near Bristol, and of Newcastle upon Tyne, and the tinminers of west Cornwall. See John Rule, *The Labouring Classes in Early Industrial England 1750–1850* (Harlow, 1986), pp. 162–6.

2 H. Rack, *Reasonable Enthusiast: John Wesley and the Rise of Methodism* (London, 1989), pp. 546–8.

3 J. H. Newman, *An Essay in Aid of Grammar of Assent* (London, 1870), p. 391. He is referring at the same time to the *Apologia*, where the relevant passage is on p. 181 in the modern edition by J. M. Cameron (London, 1973). There Newman points out that only some people are convinced by Paley's assertion that God governs the world.

4 Ibid., p. 392.

5 This is the principal thesis of Anthony Fletcher's *Gender, Sex and Subordination in England 1500–1800* (Yale, 1995).

6 Robert Southey, *The Life of Wesley*, ed. C. C. Southey (London, 1846), vol. II, pp. 433–4. This edition not only contained Knox's essay, but also S. T. Coleridge's previously unpublished comments on what Southey wrote.

7 F. Baker (ed.), *The Works of John Wesley* (Oxford, 1982), vol. XXVI p. 415.

8 Rack, *Reasonable Enthusiast*, p. 539.

9 Southey, *Life of Wesley*, vol. II, p. 147.

10 Baker, *Works of John Wesley*, vol. XXVI, p. 415.

11 Ibid., p. 416.

12 Ibid., p. 391.

13 Ibid., p. 408.

14 Ibid., p. 391.

15 Paul Langford, *Public Life and the Propertied Englishman 1689–1798* (Oxford, 1991).

16 John Rule discusses the so-called 'negative effect' of Methodism on working-class people in J. Rule, R. Wells, *Crime, Protest and Popular Politics in Southern England* (London, 1997), pp. 70–8, but much of this is a discussion about Cornwall, and about teetotalism, which belongs to the nineteenth century and was not deeply established in Wesleyanism.

17 Rule, *Labouring Classes*, pp. 220–2.

18 J. Barker-Benfield, *The Culture of Sensibility* (Chicago, 1992).

19 Cennick's papers are at Moravian Church House in London.

20 There are many examples of Boswell's habit in his journals. See, for example, J. W. Reed (ed.), *Boswell, Laird of Auchinleck, 1778–82* (New York, 1977), pp. 77–95.

21 Nicholas Rogers, 'Crowd and People in the Gordon Riots', in E. Hellmuth (ed.), *The Transformation of Political Culture* (Oxford, 1991).

22 Ibid., p. 53.

23 Mary E. Fissell, 'Charity Universal? Institutions and Moral Reform in Eighteenth-Century Bristol', in L. Davison (ed.), *Stilling the Grumbling Hive* (Sutton, 1992), p. 140.

Select bibliography

Baker, F. (ed.), *The Works of John Wesley* (Oxford, 1982), vol. XXVI.
  John Wesley and the Church of England (London, 1970).
Barker-Benfield, J., *The Culture of Sensibility* (Chicago, 1992).
Barry, J., Morgan, K. (eds.), *Reformation and Revival in Eighteenth-
  Century Bristol* (Bristol Record Society, 1994).
Beckerlegge, D. A., Hildebrandt, F. (eds.), *The Works of John Wesley*
  (London, 1983) vol. VII.
Bermingham, A., Brewer, J. (eds.), *The Consumption of Culture 1660–
  1800* (London, 1997).
Bradley, J. E., 'The Anglican Pulpit, the Social Order, and the Resur-
  gence of Toryism during the American Revolution', in *Albion*,
  1989, vol. 21.
Brantley, R. E., *Locke, Wesley and the Method of English Romanticism*
  (Florida, 1984).
Brown, E. K., *Women of Mr Wesley's Methodism* (New York, 1983).
Chilcote, P. W., *John Wesley and the Women Preachers of Early
  Methodism* (London, 1991).
Clark, J., *English Society 1688–1832* (Cambridge, 1985).
  *Samuel Johnson: Literature, Religion and English Cultural Politics
  from the Restoration to Romanticism* (Cambridge, 1994).
Colley, L., *Britons, Forging the Nation 1707–1837* (London, 1992).
Coward, B., *Social Change and Continuity in Modern England 1550–
  1750* (Harlow, 1988).
Cragg, G. R. (ed.), *The Works of John Wesley* (Oxford, 1975), vol. XI.
Curnock, N. (ed.), *John Wesley's Journal* (London, 1909–16, reprinted
  1938).
Davison, L. (ed.), *Stilling the Grumbling Hive* (Sutton, 1992).

Doody, M. A., *A Natural Passion: The Novels of Samuel Richardson* (Oxford, 1974).

Field, C. D., 'Religious Practice in the Diocese of Oxford', in *Southern History*, (1992) vol. 14.

    Anti-Methodist Publications of the Eighteenth Century (Bulletin of the John Rylands Library, Manchester, 1991).

Fiering, N., *Moral Philosophy at Seventeenth-Century Harvard: a Discipline in Transition* (Chapel Hill, 1981).

Fletcher, A., *Gender, Sex and Subordination in England 1500–1800* (Yale, 1995).

Green, V. H. H., *John Wesley* (London, 1964).

Harrison, P., *Religion and the 'Religions' in the English Enlightenment* (Cambridge, 1990).

Harvey, Van A., *Feuerbach and the Interpretation of Religion* (London, 1995).

Haydon, C., Taylor, S., Walsh, J. (eds.), *The Church of England 1689–1833: from Toleration to Tractarianism* (Cambridge, 1993).

Heizenrater, R. P., *Wesley and the People called Methodists* (Nashville, 1995).

Hellmuth, E. (ed.), *The Transformation of Political Culture: England and Germany in the Late Eighteenth-Century* (Oxford, 1991).

Hempton, D., *The Religion of the People: Methodism and Popular Religion 1750–1900* (London, 1996).

Hempton, D., Hill, M., *Evangelical Protestantism in Ulster Society 1740–1890* (London, 1992).

Holmes, G., Szechi, D. (eds.), *The Age of Oligarchy: Preindustrial Britain 1722–1783* (London, 1993).

Jackson, T. (ed.), *The Lives of the Early Methodist Preachers* (2 vols., London, 1846).

Jacob, W. M., *Lay People and Religion in the Early Eighteenth Century* (Cambridge, 1996).

Jago, J., *Visitation Studies of the Diocese of York 1761–1776* (London, 1997).

Johnstone, H. D. (ed.), *Music in Britain: the Eighteenth Century* (London, 1990).

Jones, A. E., 'Protestant Dissent in Gloucestershire: a Comparison between 1676 and 1735', in *Transactions of the Bristol and Gloucester Archaeological Society* (Bristol, 1983).

Kent, J., *Holding the Fort: Studies in Victorian Revivalism* (London, 1978).

'Wesleyan Membership in Bristol 1783', in *An Ecclesiastical Miscellany* (Bristol and Gloucestershire Archaeological Society, 1976).

'John Henry Newman', in Greschat, M. (ed.), *Die Neueste Zeit* (Stuttgart, 1985).

Kimbrough, S. T., Beckerlegge, O. A., *The Unpublished Poetry of Charles Wesley* (Nashville, 1988).

King, C., Ryscamp, D. (eds.), *Letters and Prose Writings of William Cowper* (2 vols., London, 1979).

Koditschek, T., *Class Formation in Urban Industrial Society in Bradford 1750–1850* (Cambridge, 1990).

Langford, P., *Public Life and the Propertied Englishman 1689–1798* (Oxford, 1991).

Leger, A., *John Wesley's Last Love* (London, 1910).

Lehmann, D., *The Struggle for the Spirit* (London, 1996).

Lyles, A. M., *Methodism Mocked: the Satirical Reaction to Methodism in the Eighteenth Century* (London, 1960).

Macarthy, F., *William Morris* (London, 1994).

Macdonald, M., *Mystical Religion: Madness, Anxiety and Healing in Seventeenth-Century England* (Cambridge, 1981).

Mack, P., *Visionary Women* (California, 1992).

McLoughlin, W. G., *Revivals, Awakenings and Reform* (Chicago, 1978).

Newton, J., *Susanna Wesley and the Puritan Tradition in Methodism* (London, 1968).

Noll, M. A., Bebbington, D. W., Rawlyk, G. (eds.), *Evangelicalism: Comparative Studies of Popular Protestantism in North America, the British Isles and beyond, 1700–1990* (London, 1994).

Norton, R. E., *The Beautiful Soul: Aesthetic Morality in the Eighteenth Century* (Cornell, 1995).

Nussbaum, F., *The Autobiographical Subject: Gender and Ideology in Eighteenth-Century England* (Baltimore, 1989).

Outler, A. C. (ed.), *The Works of John Wesley, Sermons on Several Occasions* (Nashville, 1984) vol. I.

Priestley, J., *An Examination of Mr Hume's Dialogues on Natural Religion (1780)*, in *Hume on Natural Religion*, ed. S. Tweyman (Bristol, 1996).

Rack, H. D., *Reasonable Enthusiast: John Wesley and the Rise of Methodism* (London, 1989).

Radner, E., *The End of the Church: a Pneumatology of Christian Division in the West* (Michigan, 1998).

Ransome, M. (ed.), *Church of England Diocese of Salisbury 1782–1791: Wiltshire Returns to Visitation Enquiries 1783* (Wiltshire Record Society, 1972).

Reed, J. W. (ed.), *Boswell, Laird of Auchinleck, 1778–1782* (New York, 1977).

Rivers, I., *Reason, Grace and Sentiment: a Study of the Language of Religion and Ethics in England 1660–1780* (Cambridge, 1991).

Rule, J., *The Labouring Classes in Early Industrial England 1750–1850* (Harlow, 1986).

Rule, J., Wells, R., *Crime, Protest and Popular Politics in Southern England* (London, 1997).

Rupp, E. G., *Religion in England 1688–1791* (Oxford, 1986).

Sack, J. J., *From Jacobite to Conservative: Reaction and Orthodoxy in Britain, 1760–1832* (Cambridge, 1993).

Schmidt, M., *John Wesley: a Theological Biography*, trans. Inman, D. (London, 1973).

Semmel, B., *The Methodist Revolution* (London, 1974).

Skinner, J., *The Journal of a Somerset Rector 1803–1834*, ed. Coombs, H., Coombs, P. (Oxford, 1971).

Spadafora, D., *The Idea of Progress in Eighteenth-Century Britain* (Yale, 1990).

Spurr, J., *The Restoration of the Church of England 1645–1689* (Yale, 1991).

Sullivan, R. E., *John Toland and the Deist Controversy* (Cambridge, Mass., 1982).

Telford, J. (ed.), *The Letters of John Wesley* (London, 1931).

Vasey, D. (ed.), *The Diary of Thomas Turner 1754–1765* (Oxford, 1984).

Vickers, J., *Thomas Coke, Apostle of Methodism* (London, 1969).

Walpole, H., *Correspondence*, ed. Lewis, W. S. (Yale, 1961), vol. XXXI.

Walsh, J., 'Origins of the Evangelical Revival', in *Essays in Modern Church History*, ed. Bennett, G. V., Walsh, J. D. (London, 1966.)

Ward, W. R., *The Protestant Evangelical Awakening* (London, 1992). *Faith and Faction* (London, 1993).

Ward, W. R., Heizenrater, R. P., *Journal and Diaries of John Wesley* (Nashville, 1988–99).

Index